"*Black Capitalists* asks what changes about contemporary capitalism when practiced while being Black. Dr. Laryea answers with transatlantic evidence recruited from street sales and glassy high-floor offices. Few scholars have worked so many different ways to get real about economic experience. This is a powerful book staging an important conversation."
—Kathryn Lofton, author of *Consuming Religion*

"*Black Capitalists* is more than a book—it's a mirror, a map, and a call to build. Dr. Laryea stitches together history and ambition, showing us that wealth is not just about accumulation but about transformation. Within these pages, you'll find stories of resilience, lessons etched in both triumph and trial, and a Black Print™—a wisdom passed down, refined, and made new for those daring enough to dream in color."
—Alloysius Attah, CEO of Farmerline and partner of Fund7

"The myth of Black Capitalism has been examined. Dr. Laryea deftly examines the reality. She redefines, reimagines, and repositions Black Capitalism in a way that sparkles, inspires, and intrigues—a must-read."
—Keith Errol Benson, GRAMMY Award–winning artist and senior fellow at Harvard University

"An honest, unflinching engagement with modern-day capitalism, its harms, and its promise, *Black Capitalists* is creative nonfiction at its very best."
—Rachel Godsil, Distinguished Professor of Law, Rutgers Law School, and cofounder of Perception Institute

"*Black Capitalists* is the story of unique individuals, innovators, and entrepreneurs of all backgrounds. Dr. Laryea's personal story reflects grit, resourcefulness, and determination to succeed against the odds. She took her learnings from the Tsai Center for Innovative Thinking at Yale (Tsai CITY) and provided insights into making capitalist systems more inclusive."
—Joe Tsai, chairman of Alibaba Group and founder of Tsai CITY

Black Capitalists

A Blueprint for What Is Possible

Rachel Laryea, PhD

CROWN
NEW YORK

CROWN
An imprint of the Crown Publishing Group
A division of Penguin Random House LLC
1745 Broadway
New York, NY 10019
crownpublishing.com
penguinrandomhouse.com

Library of Congress Cataloging-in-Publication Data
has been applied for.

Hardcover ISBN 978-0-593-73504-6
Ebook ISBN 978-0-593-73505-3

Editor: Libby Burton and Aubrey Martinson
Editorial assistant: Cierra Hinckson
Production editor: Joyce Wong
Text designer: Andrea Lau
Production: Heather Williamson
Copy editor: Gwen Colvin
Proofreaders: Janet Renard, Eldes Tran
Indexer: J S Editorial, LLC
Publicist: Stacey Stein
Marketer: Chantelle Walker

Manufactured in the United States of America

9 8 7 6 5 4 3 2 1

First Edition

The authorized representative in the EU for product safety and compliance
is Penguin Random House Ireland, Morrison Chambers, 32 Nassau Street,
Dublin D02 YH68, Ireland, https://eu-contact.penguin.ie.

AUTHOR'S NOTE

Black Capitalists is nonfiction. The ethnography of this book was conducted between 2015 and 2024. All quotations were either captured by a physical or digital recorder or copied from official documents. The names of some family members and professionals have been changed to protect their privacy. The opinions expressed here belong solely to me and do not reflect the views of JPMorganChase.

To my grandparents, for who and what they left behind.

A good man leaves an inheritance to his children's children,
but the sinner's wealth is laid up for the righteous.
—PROVERBS 13:22,
ENGLISH STANDARD VERSION

CONTENTS

INTRODUCTION

Secure the Bag
and the People

I've been curious about Black wealth for as long as I can remember. I grew up with unusual access to spaces of privilege, although I lacked authority in them. Throughout my childhood my family lived from paycheck to paycheck with a string of government assistance programs filling in the gap. Affordable housing benefits and free and reduced meals through the public school system were the most common. Just rich enough to be poor in white suburbia, I saw the kinds of wealth old money produces. When I entered my predominantly white college preparatory school as a Black scholarship student, I saw the opportunities that come with monetary resources, powerful networks, and pedigree. I always wondered what it could mean to be both Black *and* rich—and what it would cost.

My mother migrated to the United States from Ghana in 1988 where she left a comfortable life in search of the American Dream. Although she was a trained baker in Accra, her credentials were not acknowledged in the United States. So she took two minimum-wage jobs as a security officer, working the grave-yard shift in airports and office buildings, because that's what was available to her as a single Black mother of two children. But what she lacked in money she made up for in social capital as she built a network of ambitious migrants and rich white people who advised her on ways to create stability for her family.

She bought her first home, a navy-blue-and-white town-house, in the most affluent county of Northern Virginia with the help of a government-sponsored affordable housing program. So my brother, Dash, and I grew up in a white suburban neighborhood with picturesque white-picket fences, nuclear families, and recreation centers, as well as fully funded public schools with overzealous parent-teacher associations.

My mom instilled in us the belief that education was the way out of poverty and limited life options and into the American Dream that my white neighbors in a small town called South Riding seemed to have been born into. My brother and I became comrades in the journey to "get out." As the younger sibling, I benefited from all of the life experimenting he had to do as a first-generation everything.

Turns out our mom was right: Education was the way out of poverty. Dash and I are now both home-owning Yale graduates with handsome finance salaries. Occasionally, we joke about what it took to get out (in short, the "failure is not an option" mentality instilled by our mother), but most of our conversations on the topic now center on how to *stay* out. Maximizing opportunities, investing, and building our own businesses are some of the ways we talk about and imagine long-term economic stability for ourselves and our shared family, while never losing sight of the racial, health, and safety costs of Black poverty.

Growing up, I got along well with my white friends in elementary and middle school by learning how they talked, their cultural sensibilities, and what mattered to them. But the imposter syndrome I felt crept in through our material differences, which I desperately tried to hide. I made sure I was the last one to get my cafeteria lunch because I didn't want people to know that I received free and reduced-price meals. And although we took the school bus together five days a week, I walked the long way home so that no one knew exactly where I lived. I was ashamed that my family's subsidized four-bedroom row house paled in comparison to the mansions my classmates called home.

I blamed the shame of living in poverty on my Blackness because every depiction I saw of wealth was associated with whiteness. My thirteen-year-old mind thought that my Black identity had everything to do with my family's socioeconomic status, and I hated the isolation I thought my race had created.

The cognitive dissonance intensified when I attended a $60,000-a-year, single-sex college preparatory boarding school on a full-ride academic scholarship provided by the Jack Kent Cooke Foundation. I struggled to find my footing in a place that I was *in* due to merit, but not *of* due to my class and economic position. Later, while in college at NYU, I was recruited to intern at Goldman Sachs. I knew nothing about finance or economics as a social and cultural analysis major, but I did know what it meant to not have money. So having access to it—*lots of it*—was reason enough to navigate yet another space I was *in* but not *of*.

I worked at Goldman Sachs not out of interest in the financial markets, but out of a desire to graduate debt free. A job on Wall Street ensured this financial freedom. After college graduation, I returned for full-time employment intending not to climb the corporate ladder, but to cobble together a safety net wide enough to rationalize later pursuing a precarious livelihood in academia.

During my second year of graduate school, I launched a quirky food business that produces vegan plantain-based treats. This labor of love was inspired by my passion for using cultural foods as a vehicle for community-making, healthy eating, and celebrating my roots. To this day, I owe the American Dream to my mother, my extended family, and my community an ocean away. It's why I returned to the financial industry after graduate school despite its many contradictions.

Wall Street is an exclusive industry, largely composed of white males. However, research proves that diversity of all types increases profit, and some top-tier banks have committed themselves to global diversity initiatives geared toward the recruitment and retention of Black talent—a demographic with consistently low retention numbers. Despite official policies aimed at increasing the number of Black professionals at the junior level, studies show that little has changed over the past few decades. Employment for marginalized populations on Wall Street is still often marked by limited career mobility, limited access to lucrative work assignments, and limited management opportunities. So much so some Black professionals are turning elsewhere; many looking to Africa, and Ghana specifically, as an entrepreneurial incubator to apply their financial acumen, monetary resources, and social capital derived from their Wall Street careers.

Ghana's long-standing effort to bridge the gap between the Black American, European, African, Caribbean, and Latin experience through Pan-Africanism—a movement that aims to build solidarity between indigenous people and diasporans of the African continent—has yielded positive results. Known in recent years as a tourist destination for Black travelers, the country has become an attractive place for Black people to visit and live without concern for their physical safety as intolerance for racism and police brutality in America grows. Ghana's civility, economic potential, and embrace of the global Black community is pulling thousands of Black people back to the continent while reversing the effects of brain drain created by the Atlantic slave trade and sustained through modern migratory patterns. More than ever before, the children of African immigrants and the descendants of enslaved Black people living in America and beyond are looking to Ghana to realize America's democratic ideals of life, liberty, and the pursuit of happiness.

But my tenure at Goldman Sachs is what exposed me to elite Black social life for the first time. I met others with similar stories who carry their own social debts, desires, and fears, and who fascinated me by their ability to adopt tactical behaviors and mindsets that ensured their personal and professional success in a predominantly white space rampant with structural racism and inequality.

My early days on Wall Street also made me aware of an unsettling personal truth I couldn't ignore. I was ashamed of not having money growing up, but when I got it, I was ashamed of *where* and *how* I got it. The source of my newly acquired wealth came from "the dark side"—a pejorative term my classmates who pursued arguably more altruistic careers used to describe corporate America, with Wall Street being "the belly of the beast."

Black Capitalist and Black Capitalism Defined

Some scholars of Black and African studies have long argued that while Black people were the labor force that built the infrastructure of American capitalism through the violent enforcement of legalized slavery, we cannot, and should not, aspire to be the beneficiaries of it. This is thanks to structural racism, the destructive features of the political economy (the theory and practice of economic affairs in relation to society and politics), and the belief that capitalism is incapable of producing true social good. To thrive within capitalism comes at the expense of diminishing someone else's life chances through exploitative practices. So it's better to collectively resist the system and persevere through the struggles that come with that.

Many of the Black Capitalists I encountered did not disagree with this sentiment. In fact, they were highly critical of modern-day capitalism. But they were simultaneously unapologetic about using capitalist strategies in the service of a social agenda that favors Black people. Informed by their stories, I define a Black Capitalist as a Black person who is a strategic participant of capitalism with the intention to benefit from the political economy in order to create social good. But it's not just Black people who can have a socially restorative mindset when thinking and behaving in capitalism.

I define Black Capitalism as a pragmatic theory that accounts for the ways actors, individual and collective, proactively reposition themselves within capitalism to achieve social good. These definitions, which prioritize social good *and* monetary profit, are crucial to how I make the case for the creation of a more equitable version of capitalism throughout this book. The point is not simply to occupy a more powerful position within capitalism, but to participate in capitalism in such a way that engenders social good for others, and limits the exploitation that capitalism, as we know it, is built upon. According to this framework, being Black and/or actively engaged in capitalism doesn't inherently make someone a practitioner of Black Capitalism.

One must repeatedly choose to have a communal mindset and remain committed to advancing social good.

These definitions also reveal how Black is both a racial status and a social position. Adopting a Black Capitalist identity indicates one's affinity to a racial group, whereas practicing Black Capitalism, which is race agnostic, acknowledges Black people's distinct economic experience in America, which is shaped by structural racism, and the acts of solidarity required by everyone to build a new kind of capitalism aimed to benefit all.

The more time I spent with these Black Capitalists on Wall Street, I saw that their approach was intriguing, complicated, practical, and riddled with contradictions. It made me curious. Where is the space for Black Capitalist thriving?

My experiences dating to childhood led me to write this book. I learned that the price of Blackness is both social and economic. This book is a story about how race makes a difference in how we experience and participate in capitalism—and how that difference teaches all of us something about how to build a version of capitalism that ensures collective thriving. We inherited a broken political economy that leaves many feeling disempowered and uncertain about their ability to unlock financial freedom in their lifetime. The global stories of the Black Capitalists in this book are a blueprint for how we can secure the bag *and* the people.

"Black Capitalists Don't Exist!"

To many, the term *Black Capitalists* is oxymoronic at best and problematic at worst. Its usage tiptoes into dangerous territory when the word *capitalist* is adopted and the material harms of capitalism are ignored. I learned through years of interviewing hundreds of people about their views on capitalism that some question if Black Capitalists even exist. An exchange I had with a fellow Yale colleague years ago sheds light on why some reject the possibility of a Black Capitalist identity—for themselves and others.

At the end of the second year of my doctoral program, I presented a research prospectus to an audience of my peers and faculty. Listeners sat crowded around the large wooden table in the Gordon Parks Room of Yale's African American Studies Department on 81 Wall Street. As I stood behind the podium in the corner of the room, I began my ten-minute talk with the title of my work, "Black Capitalists in the Transatlantic Financial Industry." My presentation was followed by a question-and-answer period, for which I felt prepared; however, the first comment took me by surprise. A sixth-year Black PhD candidate piped up and with disbelief in her eyes simply said: "Black Capitalists don't exist! Given the history of American capitalism, it's impossible for Black Capitalists to exist. At best they can be Black financiers, but not Capitalists."

After silently searching for the question in her direct statement while scanning the quiet room of scholars eagerly awaiting my response, I finally spoke. I said that my use of the term *Black Capitalists* reflected how my interlocutors describe themselves. I thought that was enough to placate her discontent—and quite frankly, it should have been—but the dissatisfaction on her face told me that I had not answered the question to her liking. I took my seat as the next presenter began their talk on the legacy of American slavery and the prison industrial complex, which was well received.

Put differently, what my colleague was saying was that to be Black and adopt American capitalism as one's preferred economic model presents an unresolvable contradiction: claiming affinity to a system built by enslaved Black people that has been structurally engineered to exclude Black people as the primary beneficiary of their labor. To be a Black Capitalist is to be in an identity crisis.

But witnessing the social lives of Black Capitalists in high finance shaped what I knew to be true about their existence, even if others refused to accept it because of rigid ideas about who gets to be a capitalist due to the origins of American capitalism. The truth is, you don't have to be a Black professional on Wall Street churning the wheels of capitalism to be one of its many actors. No matter our station in life, we are all participating in capitalism and have some choice as to *how* we show up. The Black Capitalist is not just the person in the white collared shirt sitting behind a double monitor in a high-rise office. She can be the person selling you ChapStick and T-shirts while braiding your hair at the salon, or the man in the streets of Accra creating dozens of monetary transactions every day. The *gig economy* is just a modern term for what Black people have been doing all along.

I've learned that the meaning of capitalism itself changes depending on whom you ask. Within Black populations, it is largely informed by culture, survival entrepreneurship within gig and informal economies, and the historical, intergenerational legacy of structural barriers to generational wealth building. Given this, it's no surprise that when I ask Black people what capitalism means to them, the common responses are "the root of all evil," "a tool built by the white man to keep us down," and a "system that needs to be dismantled."

These responses reveal the two main power positions within a capitalist economy—the capitalist and the laborer. We are well acquainted with the laborer position and its extractive and exploitative tendencies. Given the structural racism responsible for driving the racial wealth gap in America today, it's no coincidence that white people are both the greatest producers of capitalist markets and recipients of the system.

But here's a definition that will work for our purposes: Capitalism is a political economy in which private actors own the means of production to freely create and sell commodities, with intent to yield excess capital. Who gets to be a private actor or a capitalist in this case? Anyone. That's both hopeful and worrisome. Hopeful in that this definition of capitalism makes room for us to discard the racialized position of capitalist and laborer. Yes, there are profound barriers to accessing capital for marginalized groups, as white people have long been the gatekeepers and the primary beneficiaries. But that does not mean marginalized groups are inherently unable to amass capital and engage in capitalism as private actors. If capitalism is to be more than the snake eating its tail, it must be a system that benefits all—and not only the few.

◆ ◆ ◆

Toward the end of graduate school, I grew disillusioned by academia writ large and questioned the quality of life I could afford as a newly minted doctor of philosophy in a bleak job market. So I went back to what I knew and what pays—finance. But this time, it would be at JPMorganChase. On the heels of George Floyd's murder, the firm, like many others, made a public vow to fight racial inequity. This promise, the Racial Equity Commitment (REC), was worth $30 billion. The five-year initiative catalyzed lines of businesses across the firm to establish objectives and key results in service of closing the racial wealth gap and advancing the economic futures of Black, Hispanic, and Latino communities through strategic investments that would surpass the five-year term. When I read the LinkedIn job posting for the strategist role, I was hooked.

But I was also naive. Impressed by how senior management called out the structural racism in the finance industry during my interview, I thought so much had changed since my time at Goldman Sachs. People were no longer shying away from openly talking about race and racism in the workplace. Instead, they were throwing billions of dollars toward addressing its problems. It seemed like a perfect fit at an institution heavily scrutinized for its ethics. Bearing the mental weight of all that I had learned as a researcher and entrepreneur about new forms of capitalism and the standard to which I hold myself, I thought it was a job that I could feel good about while supporting society's most economically disadvantaged population.

Less than ninety days into my new role, I reconsidered my choices. I learned that change is hard-won and never happens overnight. My team was tasked with the challenge of influencing the firm's business lines to redesign their tried-and-true ways of working. At face value, long-standing business strategies produced profit for the firm and its employees, but our job was to expose our stakeholders to potential business opportunities within Black, Hispanic, and Latino communities. Changing mindsets and behaviors shaped by habit was hard enough without the pressure of time. The further removed the world became from the day of George Floyd's murder, the harder it became to maintain the momentum that prompted the firm's action.

Then on June 29, 2023, the U.S. Supreme Court voted to end affirmative action in higher education on the grounds that it violated the Equal Protection Clause of the Fourteenth Amendment to the Constitution.[1] Rumors spread quickly about how the ruling would impact our work. Internal legal counsel spent weeks conducting their due diligence, and though little changed in our day-to-day operations, it was a tense time. My team's managing director advised our regional leadership to refrain from publicly speculating about the firm's commitment to racial equity after the completion of the REC while the dust settled and the firm's lawyers ensured the company's protection.

I witnessed the life cycle of a Diversity, Equity, and Inclusion (DEI) initiative from the vantage point of a DEI practitioner for the first time. But simultaneous progress and regress made about racial equity in this country is not unprecedented. We've been here before. The birth of the commitment was celebrated nationwide. Its infancy was nurtured. But as time went on and society came to worrisome conclusions about the significance of race in America, its development was challenged.

This critical step backward made it that much harder to see efforts like the Racial Equity Commitment to maturity and innovate beyond them. My team's work was no longer just about advancing a socioeconomic initiative that could be perceived as inconvenient or untimely, but also mitigating the fear of exposing an organization to the possibility of legal retribution. The Supreme Court ruling gives organizations an out to write the legal risk off as unnecessary and back away from championing equity work altogether. Thankfully, Jamie Dimon, the CEO of JPMorganChase, continued to defend DEI work while other CEOs went silent. In his 2023 letter to shareholders, in which he reflected on the company's position on its DEI programs, Dimon noted: "We're thoughtfully continuing our diversity, equity and inclusion efforts. Of course, JPMorganChase will conform as the laws evolve. We will scour our programs, our words, and our actions to make sure they comply. That said, we think all the efforts . . . will remain largely unchanged."[2] The reasons for this decision were that these efforts are embraced by cities and communities around the world, and that, as Dimon put it, the firm's DEI initiatives "make us a more inclusive company and lead to more innovation, smarter decisions and better financial results for us and for the economy as well."[3]

Even still, I was depressed by it all. I struggled to overcome the challenge of staying motivated when what was called into question was much more than the continuance of a commitment. My humanity was on the line as a Black woman doing work to close the racial wealth gap that kept Black people behind in critical areas such as homeownership, small business development, and financial literacy. The legal "scouring" of this work forced me to reckon with my duality. I was a JPMC employee developing strategies to deploy the firm's commitment in cities across the country, but I was also a JPMC customer benefiting from the initiatives that were now under the microscope.

Everyday Black Capitalists—those not among the elite—acquire capital and use it to empower and sustain their local and global communities while creating a blueprint for collective Black economic security. This book traces the socially conscious pursuit of Black thriving through the means of capitalism. Critical race theory taught in the academy and the collective Black consciousness that exists outside of it both posit that capitalism is inherently problematic and is designed to oppress marginalized peoples. But that's not the only story.

This is why Black social practices, such as the Pan-African holiday Kwanzaa, have included economic components. In Kwanzaa, the fourth principle, Ujamaa, stands for cooperative economics: "To build and maintain our own stores, shops and other businesses and to profit from them together."[4] Additionally, with millionaire status on the rise internationally, there is a groundswell effort within the Black community to democratize knowledge on financial health, investing savviness, and generational wealth building. Telling global stories of Black Capitalism—as I will here—draws our attention to the nuanced ways Black people are participating in capitalism and counters the prevailing narrative that the only relationship Black people can have to capitalism is to be exploited.

Throughout these chapters I share some of my most sobering, rewarding, and complicated experiences as the child of African immigrants, a Wall Street professional, a Yale-trained anthropologist and Black studies scholar, and a *New York Times*–featured entrepreneur. By weaving in the stories and theories of capitalist thriving among my family members, my friends, and the Black and African professionals who enrich the ethnography of this book, I uncover the important truth that, much like Black people, the Black Capitalist experience is not monolithic. The multiple forms and practices of Black Capitalism reveal the underlying desires and fears that keep us entangled with capitalism, as well as the nuanced engagements within capitalism aimed to create a more equitable world.

Again, where is the space for Black Capitalist thriving? There are many spaces, but this book tracks the unexpected and overlooked ones: professional life on Wall Street; social trends amplifying hustle culture and the soft life; entrepreneurship and the gig economy throughout Africa and the diaspora; and representations of prominent Black people in popular culture, television, and film. These spaces share a focus on Black identity, wealth creation, and capitalism. But beyond pinpointing the presence of Black Capitalism in various spaces, this book calls our attention to the significance of race in our effort to better understand our political economy as it functions today and how we might change it for the better. There is tension in the interplay between race and money. And much like life's biggest questions, these tensions are never fully resolved. But confronting them and the discomfort they carry makes us better equipped to leverage capitalism in service of collective social good.

The Racial Tax on Thriving

In the fall of 2024, I was invited by the Columbia Business School to give a talk about my research to an audience of students and faculty. It would be my first time presenting my work to a non-Yale audience, and I was straight-up scared. Management scholars, economists, historians, sociologists, anthropologists, and others have long been fascinated by capitalism. And because of this, there are many entry points to studying it. Some have taken genealogical approaches; others have considered how capitalism informs and affects the interconnected relationships between the state, society, corporations, and the environment at varying levels of scale. Others still research the multiple forms of capitalism that exist today in an effort to assess the promise and problems of our economic system. So what would be my entry point? My Yale prospectus presentation proved that my research is an emotional topic capable of triggering the intergenerational economic trauma many Black people experience. I knew that if I was going to pursue telling what I know to be a hopeful story with a long narrative arc, I needed to first tell the darkest and most painful parts of the story to acknowledge the trauma many of us carry in order to then lead us forward.

As I was preparing my lecture, I came across an image that caused me to pause. It was a photograph of a man of color with his back against a white cement wall on which a sentence appeared in red spray-painted capital letters: "EVERY MORNING I WAKE UP ON THE WRONG SIDE OF CAPITALISM." The word that drew me in was "I." It made me wonder: What about one's identity can create the feeling of living on the wrong side of capitalism? Race is one of the core cultural identifiers that creates such a feeling for many. It did for me as a thirteen-year-old girl who blamed my Black identity for the poverty in which I lived.

A common saying is "You can't have capitalism without racism." This is the crux of one of the many entry points—and the one that I use—to a study of capitalism called *racial capitalism*. It's a popularized literature and theoretical framework that draws conclusions about the relationship between race and our economic system. A review of the scholarship is the best place to start because the key topics within the literature explain the features of racial capitalism. But it's not where we'll stay because much of the scholarship is limited in its imagination of the relationship between race and class. I use racial capitalism and its related literature simply as a way to connect this work to history, acknowledge some of the most popular thinking done on race and class, and challenge it to create new forms of thinking.

Racial capitalism has three prevailing claims. First, capitalism is inherently racialized because it exploits race (among other socially constructed differences) in order to function. Second, capitalism is experienced through difference. And third, capitalism cannot exist without its dependency on socially constructed difference.[5] The rigidity of these claims, paired with the commonly held belief rooted in historical evidence that "you can't have capitalism without racism," limits who gets to wake up the *right* side of capitalism. Although the history that underwrites this framework cannot be ignored, we also cannot ignore the ways Black people are actively engaging with capitalism, not squarely as exploited capital to be wielded for institutional use, but as the drivers of production with objectives that complicate prevailing and reductive narratives about capitalists and the spectrum of their intentions.

A common critique to my challenge of racial capitalism are the famous words of Audre Lorde: "The master's tools will never dismantle the master's house."[6] As a feminist, civil rights activist, and self-described "warrior," Lorde made unquestionable contributions to the Black radical tradition.[7] But the popular quote makes me curious. Specific to Black Capitalism, what are the "tools," and can they be repurposed to serve new ends? Is the finality of "never" truly warranted? If the house can't be dismantled with the master's tools, is there room at least to reimagine its design and construction? Can diverse practices of Black Capitalism, the blueprint for a new kind of capitalism aimed to ensure collective economic thriving, effect long-lasting change? What we lose in Lorde's words is the perspective that everything evolves with time, including capitalism. Lorde's theoretical framework was fit for the time in which she lived. But how do we update our thinking and practice to account for *this* time and capitalism's evolution in direct response to our resistance?

To answer these questions, it's important to put Lorde's statement in context. In 1979, Lorde was invited by New York University to give comments on feminist papers focused on difference in the lives of American women at the Institute for the Humanities conference. She offered a scathing review about the lack of attention to difference—such as race, sexuality, class, and age—that was evident in the papers: "It is a particular academic arrogance to assume any discussion of feminist theory without examining our many differences, and without a significant input from poor women, Black and Third World women, and lesbians. . . . What does it mean when the tools of a racist patriarchy are used to examine the fruits of that same patriarchy?"[8] In Lorde's view, using the tools of the system to examine the outputs of that system shrinks the boundaries for change making.[9] She concludes with a powerful message:

> Those of us who stand outside the circle of this society's definition of acceptable women; those of us who have been forged in the crucibles of difference—those of us who are poor, who are lesbians, who are Black, who are older—know that survival is not an academic skill. It is learning how to take our differences and make them strengths. For the master's tools will never dismantle the master's house. They may allow us temporarily to beat him at his own game, but they will never enable us to bring about genuine change. And this fact is only threatening to those women who still define the master's house as their only source of support.[10]

The context justifies Lorde's appraisal: A thorough analysis of the outcomes of a racist patriarchy cannot be achieved when the "tools" used to assess those outcomes include the exclusion of others and the re-centering of whiteness. There are inherent issues in creating this kind of academic feminism that would otherwise be a worthy challenge to the racist patriarchy it aims to dismantle. The transformative potential of this feminist effort is rendered moot because of its poor design and execution. Hence Lorde's cautionary tale. To be both fully *in* and *of* the master's house threatens one's ability to change it despite the best of intentions.

But when I consider Lorde's speech through the lens of Black Capitalism, the change-making limits Lorde warns Black people of wobbles in the world we have now. The stories I share throughout this book about Black Capitalists and the tools they use to create a more equitable world introduce new questions into Lorde's central argument that the tools of oppression cannot upend structures of oppression and engender change. To be Black—"forged in the crucibles of difference" and "stand[ing] outside the circle of this society's definition of acceptable"— requires a persistent "learning [of] how to take our differences and make them strengths" in order to not only survive but also collectively thrive.

It's in the duality of outsider-as-Black, and insider-as-Capitalist that Black Capitalists are able to construct a fortress of protection within the "master's house" of capitalism without naively "defin[ing] the master's house as their only source of support." Again, race makes a difference. Strategic Black participation in capitalism may not utterly "dismantle the master's house" in our lifetime, but it can, as has already been proved, make the house more equitable and just, catalyzing incremental transformation. Evident in the lives of many Black Capitalists, the conscious use of the tools of capitalism can create new conditions of possibility to both "beat him [the master] at his own game" and "enable us to bring about genuine change."

We can acknowledge that capitalism as we know it today exploits race, is experienced through difference, and is sustained through difference while also expanding our ideas about who gets to be the beneficiaries of capitalist production and how—Black Capitalists *do* exist. Recognizing that race creates a difference in how people participate in capitalism allows us to identify opportunities to create more equitable practices within it. This book intervenes in the literature of racial capitalism by proposing an alternative relation between Black people and capitalism: prosperous, productive, and liberating.

And it considers the variable meanings of *race* for Black American and African diasporic groups. As I mentioned before, a Black identity indicates both a racial distinction and a social position.[11] Blackness is socially constructed as a physical feature that people see and often use as a way to consciously or subconsciously categorize others into social hierarchies of power. The benchmark for this hierarchy is whiteness, otherwise known as "the norm" and substantiated through institutionalized racism. All other racial identities become deviations from the norm, which bears implications on how one is treated in society.

Blackness as a racial distinction and social position is experienced everywhere. A common misconception is that race does not exist outside of America and especially not on the African continent, where in most countries the majority of people are considered Black. When we zoom into an American context, we can pinpoint how the social construction of race, which ironically followed the creation of racism (to justify the practice of racism), negatively affected the economic lives of Black people during the Atlantic slave trade and beyond. When we zoom out to a global context, we also see how international actors once perceived—during the height of colonialism—and still perceive Africa as a site for extraction and exploitation due to problematic beliefs held about the majority of people who occupy the continent.

There was a time in American history when the definition of race was so fluid that certain people who are considered white today once were not. During the late 1800s and into the early 1900s, when Poles, Hungarians, Italians, Slavs, Greeks, and other Europeans immigrated to America, they weren't considered white on sight. They had to "earn" their whiteness, and the privileges that come with it, through the practice of respectability politics. And until then, they were stuck in limbo—below the social standing of white people and above that of Blacks.

What's important is that the global melting pot that we know as America created the opportunity for certain immigrant groups to change—and in this case, "elevate"—their race distinction and social status while denying that opportunity to others. Black Americans and Africans have remained Black racially and have been locked into the lowest social position through structural racism. The tax on Blackness has been both permanent and global in reach. Through my story and that of others, this book considers the interconnected experience of what it means for Black people living in America to be Black while coming from different geographic backgrounds in our shared desire to enhance our socioeconomic position.

The last area of focus that I anchor this book in is the study of entrepreneurship. It's a topic that I'll delve deeply into in chapter 3, where I discuss hustle culture. But for now, although much is written about entrepreneurship, little is said about Black entrepreneurship within the field of racial capitalism. It's a phenomenon that's largely overlooked because the focus within the literature is on theorizing Black bodies as forms of capital rather than the agents of capital production. This book, and the diverse stories of Black entrepreneurship throughout it, is a reflection of my investment in creating more intellectual space to consider

Black productivity, ingenuity, and creativity on a global scale. My pivot toward a Black entrepreneurial approach to the study of racial capitalism does not ignore the material constraints imposed on Black people during the antebellum and postbellum periods; rather, it underscores the Black entrepreneur's resilience, creativity, and relentless desire for self-fashioning that is often lost in a literature focused on the rigid and exploitative relation between Black people and capitalism.

As an anthropologist and scholar of Black studies, my North Star is telling stories that center Black life and bridge the gap between how people narrate their lives and how the world they live in receives them. Writing this story about elite and everyday Black Capitalists to capture the expansiveness and complexity of Black life is one step toward my guiding light. What follows is a close examination of people who make the most out of an imperfect political economy to secure prosperity for themselves and their communities. My study of how and why Black Capitalists do what they do is not an attempt to judge individual or collective choices. Doing so would be irrelevant and get in the way of producing knowledge from which we can all learn and grow. What matters most in these pages is the new set of questions and exciting possibilities this story uncovers about Black participation in modern-day capitalism, and the opportunity we have to create a world in which we can all wake up on the right side of capitalism.

PART I

The American Dream

CHAPTER 1

A Long Way
from Adams Drive

I first learned I was both Black and poor around the same time during my childhood. Although my grandmother raised me in Accra, Ghana, for a few years following my birth in 1993, my first recollection of home was 69 Adams Drive, a tan, two-story row house with a shabby roof made of charcoal-colored shingles and a single white plastic chair placed next to the front door. The lawn looked as if rain hadn't come to that part of Leesburg, Virginia, for a long time. A mocha-colored fence missing most of its pickets hugged the house and the hard stubbly ground it stood on.

The neighborhood had the same feel as my home—modest and worn yet adequate. The Black neighbors exchanged pleasantries and shared a smoke from time to time, while the few white and Latino residents kept to themselves. Given my mom's insistence that I come straight home after school, I rarely saw the violence that incited the police sirens that often interrupted my sleep. Sometimes I'd see the aftermath in the form of slashed car tires on my morning walk to the bus stop.

My dad was often found sitting on his front-porch chair drinking a Heineken six-pack with a box of Camel cigarettes nearby, chewing raw ginger while chatting with his high school classmates on the phone, or fast asleep in his cedar recliner that was the eyesore of our cramped living room. He sat there so frequently that the chair's headrest had a permanent round grease stain from the pomade he used for his balding scalp. I liked to think that his physical presence made up for his emotional absence in my life before my parents' divorce and his exit from the remainder of my childhood.

Our mornings started at four-thirty when Mom would wake my older brother Dash and me to complete our daily chores: wash the bathtub, scrub and wipe down the toilet and sink on each floor, sweep the laminate kitchen floor, vacuum the stained beige carpet, and dust everything else. Our cleaning was followed by study time. Over a bowl of Honey Nut Cheerios and whole milk from the Walmart down the street, I'd review my notes on class activities from the prior day and check my homework to ensure my answers were correct. My seven-year-old self often felt as if an entire day had passed by the time I walked out the front door to catch the school bus at seven-thirty.

I'd come home to read to my mom from the free newspapers she collected during her desk security job at one of the prominent telecommunication companies in town, while she snuck in a few extra hours of sleep before her next work shift. I would begrudgingly read aloud the latest on market trends and technological advancements that I didn't understand and even the obituaries as my mom snored in response. On special days I'd be allowed to watch *Wheel of Fortune* and *Jeopardy* right before my strict eight p.m. bedtime. Whenever my mom worried Dash and I didn't have enough to do, she'd pepper our daily routine with assignments to read planet Earth pamphlets from the local library and write essays about our learnings. My mom would promise trips to Disney World for exceptional work, but I slowly learned that her proclamations were a parenting hack. To this day, my mom doesn't know where Disney World is. But back then, she knew just speaking the name could influence a child's behavior.

Despite the hours spent writing what I thought were perfect essays, I usually received a C as Mom encouraged me to work harder. Her strategy to nurture a strong work ethic in me was sometimes sneaky in this way. She knew that rather than feeling deflated by an average grade, I would be inspired to be even more thorough the next time.

Sundays were church days. Leesburg Baptist Church had an active bus ministry that would collect kids living in the downtown area for morning services. I loved going to church because it was an escape from the monotony of my usual routine. My mom allowed it because it gave her the luxury of a few hours of peace and quiet to prepare for her next overnight shift.

A year after I became a church member at eight years old, my parents divorced. My dad chose to stay, so we left. Mom won an affordable housing lottery, and we moved from our two-story row house to a two-bedroom apartment on Newberry Street thirty minutes south of Leesburg. The new five-story apartment building was part of a gated complex surrounded by a thick forest, soon to be demolished to make way for real estate development. Unlike my neighbors at 69 Adams Drive, my new neighbors were mostly white and seemingly well-to-do. One similarity between my old and new neighborhood is that the white people still kept to themselves. But on Newberry Street there were no police sirens, slashed car tires, or insistence from my mom to hurry home after school.

My mom's newly single status heightened my awareness of our financial circumstances. I now noticed she had two distinct work uniforms instead of one, the chronicle of daily purchases in the back of her checkbook to keep track of how much money we had left, and the mostly bare shelves in our refrigerator. Breakfast was usually just a glass of warm milk in my tall purple cup. There were instances in our old home when the power would go out or the water would stop running, forcing us to bathe with gallon-sized water bottles, but those moments never inspired a sense of worry. The stories other kids from the neighborhood would share during our bus rides to and from school made those moments seem normal. Life on Newberry Street was different because there wasn't the comfort of shared experience with other children who looked like me.

Despite my stomach's growls of hunger I would try to mute by pressing my arms over the noise or shifting in my school chair to divert attention, I was an eager and attentive student. By the third grade, my homeroom teacher, Mrs. Anderson, identified me as gifted, and I passed the aptitude tests to prove it. I had a particular love for math because if I knew the rules of numbers, I could always figure out the right answer. Mrs. Anderson would often have us compete in times-tables tests, and the only person who could beat me was a blond, blue-eyed boy named Austin. He was smart too—and a know-it-all. With everyone else eliminated, he and I would go toe-to-toe in the last round. I reveled in the fact that I won more than I lost. Most of the children in my third-grade class at Selden's Landing Elementary School were white. Within the four walls of that classroom I realized for myself that I was Black—beating everyone, but especially Austin, at timed multiplication tests. It meant something to know that though I was different, I could beat the best of them.

I would often regard my classmates with curiosity about how different they looked from me. My hair, braided and greased with pomade, would stick out around my whole head while Austin's shiny blond hair hung limp around his pale white face. For hours I would daydream about his home life and assume it was nothing like mine. He'd come to school in clothes the cool kids wore, like crisp polo shirts with the Abercrombie moose logo embroidered on the upper right side. Mine were usually from the Salvation Army or gifted from church members. I wished for the life I imagined he had without ever knowing his life at all. We seemed different in most ways, our race the most visible distinction. But for all my envy of the material things he had, which I attributed to his whiteness, I took pride in knowing that I lacked nothing in intelligence.

Hiding Poverty

A couple months before I started fifth grade, my mom won another affordable housing lottery. But this time it was for a three-story townhouse in South Riding, Virginia, a growing and affluent upper-middle-class community in the richest county in the state. The newly built white house with blue shutters on Flannigan Terrace would be home for the remainder of my childhood. There I lived within the cluster of townhouses that stood across the street from my school, but hardly anyone knew.

For the first time, I intentionally tried to hide from others the details of my single-parent household. A buildup of shame had accumulated in my imagination. I longed to fit in with my mostly white peers, who came from two-parent households, lived in mansions, and could afford things like the popular Motorola Razr flip phone. My dated clothes and lack of attendance at weekend parties my mom strictly forbade were evidence to most I didn't fit in. But my peers respected one thing about me despite the mystery of my background—I was smart. And because I was smart, some made favorable assumptions about my family's socioeconomic status that worked to my advantage.

One day a conversation with Ellen, my Korean American classmate, veered toward the topic of money as we whispered back and forth during science class. "Do you think *I'm* rich?" I asked, returning the question she had asked me.

"Well . . . I don't know. . . . You don't dress like us, and I have never been to your house, but probably."

Leading her to say more, I asked, "How come?"

And she replied, "Because you're really smart."

The pride I'd felt in beating Austin at times tables returned in hearing Ellen's response. I didn't play the part of the average wealthy seventh grader living in South Riding, Virginia, but my smarts—nurtured through years of four-thirty wake-up calls to study and write essays—exposed her misguided belief that intelligence was reserved for the wealthy. Holding on to my secret, I smiled to myself as Ellen went back to doodling instead of taking notes.

But maintaining the same level of mystery about my family's socioeconomic status at church was impossible. With our move to South Riding, Dash and I began attending a sister church run by a family named the Michaelsons called Fellowship Baptist Church (FBC) that was walking distance from our new home. I don't know what the pastor at Leesburg Baptist told the Michaelsons, but given the money they gifted my mom to treat us to new attire for our first Sunday service, they knew we struggled financially.

Mom dropped us off for our first day of Sunday school at FBC in outfits from Macy's. Dash made his entrance in a crisp white collared shirt, a black-and-gray tie one of the men at our former church taught him to tie, and an oversized black suit. "You'll grow into it, and it will last longer," Mom said about the pants that folded over the heel of his dress shoes and the jacket that hid his small shoulders. Whereas my new ankle-length, sleeveless pink dress, with spring flowers evenly printed throughout the fabric, actually fit me.

A few minutes into Sunday school in the renovated office building designed with foldable walls to make multiple classrooms, Pastor Michaelson came strutting into his wife's class with spirit fingers and arms raised in excitement. "Stand up, let me look at ya!" Mrs. Michaelson stopped her direction of the class in a song about Joshua and the Battle of Jericho as the room fell silent. The white children stared at one another in confusion as I slowly rose from my seat to be at eye level with the pastor and his wife. "Go on, now!" he encouraged while nodding his head. Feet planted, I resentfully turned my body ninety degrees to the left and right to give him the full outfit view he was looking for. "You're embarrassing her, honey," Mrs. Michaelson pleaded on my behalf. "Why?" her husband answered. "I bought it!" Mrs. Michaelson was right. My poverty was on full display. And unlike at school, my intelligence couldn't cover it up or erase the shame I felt.

I never knew what my mom thought about our involvement at FBC until she learned what was asked of her children. The youth pastor who pitched in with carpooling would call our house some weekends to ask if Dash and I were around to lend a hand at church. We were always free, and Mom usually agreed.

But no one else in the youth group was ever called, so "lending a hand" meant that Dash and I alone cleaned the church from pew to pulpit. Vacuuming, wiping down toilet seats, organizing the storage unit that was lit by a single lightbulb, washing Communion dishes, and dusting off bookstore Bibles was just the beginning. The youth pastor was responsible for these tasks, but when I vacuumed my way into the youth room that doubled as his office, I'd find him typing away on his computer. I didn't mind so much, since I felt indebted for the rides to church and appreciated any opportunity to be out of the house.

Mom disagreed. The moment she learned that the only children who were called to clean the church were her kids, she grabbed the phone to give the youth pastor a piece of her mind. But only after she gave me the nondiplomatic version of her spiel first.

"Ttchhww heh! What does he think this is?! If he wants to pick you to church, he should pick you. That's it! Not so that you can go clean the church. Did he ask the Romanos or the Johnsons to go clean? Did he dare pick up the phone to tell Mr. Wall that his children should come clean the church up and down? Nehvah! Mark it on the wall. . . . If he eh-vah calls this house again telling you you should come clean, you will never step foot in that church again!" she threatened, wagging her index finger in the air.

This was a lesson in how money determines what people think of me, and what people believe they can expect from me. Dash and I were singled out as the help and exploited as free Black domestic labor. When you don't have money, people can demand you do humiliating things in exchange for crumbs. The desire to have money wasn't just for comfort, it was for dignity too. I knew then that I needed a new escape from poverty. And by the end of middle school, I got my ticket out.

The Ghanaian Oreo

Following in my brother's footsteps, I applied for and received a prestigious scholarship from the Jack Kent Cooke Foundation. I applied to a handful of schools but picked the Madeira School, an all-girls college preparatory boarding school that offered me a full-ride scholarship. Although I learned many things during my time at Madeira, what stayed with me and what I can clearly see now, is that being there marked the end of the myth of the monolithic Black identity, at least for me.

At home I was Ghanaian. But to the world and certainly to my white peers, I and the other seven melanated girls in our class of seventy people were just Black. I joined the Black Student Union in search of solidarity but never felt quite comfortable or fully welcomed because of my cultural ignorance. We'd be in Black History Month planning meetings, and I'd stare blankly as my peers cheered about the idea of putting on a step show or having the dining service prepare soul food. I didn't know the latest hip-hop artists or trends that friendships were sometimes built around. And it didn't help that I had white friends. By definition, I was an Oreo: Black on the outside and white on the inside. The Black girl who "acted white," according to my Black peers. The girls who called me that didn't know that my ability to interact with our white peers came from years of learning to navigate white spaces I was *in* but not *of.* Meaningful friendships with people who didn't look like me were the occasional benefit of constantly living outside my comfort zone.

But I didn't know how to "act Black" because I didn't grow up with the same cultural education as my Black American classmates. The harrowing stories of American inequality that my mom heard about while back home in Accra were proven true when she witnessed and experienced racial atrocities as a migrant on U.S. soil. For instance, when I was an infant, my skin was fairly light. Some white people called the cops on my mom with kidnapping accusations because they couldn't believe that, with her milk-chocolate complexion, she could be the mother of a light-skinned baby.

For many African migrants like my mom, the threat of discrimination created an urgent need to distinguish themselves from the victims of racialized violence who looked just like them. My mom's strategic move into white neighborhoods, schools, and social circles led her to believe that her family was less susceptible to racial inequality as a result. And her work ethic was a far departure from the "lazy," "uneducated," and "welfare-dependent" stereotypes attributed to many Black Americans.

In my early teenage years my mom introduced me to the term *akata*. A Yoruba word, not inherently derogatory, *akata* is used derisively and generally to suggest the ratchetness and incivility of Black Americans. That word drew a distinction across racial and ethnic lines. At home, we were Ghanaians—neither Black nor American. My mom used her Ghanaian identity as a shield to distance herself and her kids from the danger attached to a Black American identity. The distance created intraracial separation but couldn't remove the underlying fear of racial discrimination from white people.

To some, I was acting white. To others, I was trying to act Black and failing at it, and my peers were quick to put me on notice. I recall a conversation with my roommate Nancy about an all-school workshop on the "Black struggle" that left me unsettled. Blond and blue eyed, with curves that made her popular among the boys at our brother school, Nancy had a unique upbringing. Her parents were white Brits who moved to Jamaica to establish a profitable resort business. Raised there for most of her young life, Nancy was immersed in Caribbean culture and proximate to the lived experiences of Black islanders. She often shared and took pride in the fact that all of her boyfriends had been Black—part of her own method in gaining credibility within Madeira's Black student population.

"What is your big Black struggle, Rachel?" she asked with her eyes rolling to the back of her head. Four of the seven other Black girls in our class sat within earshot of her question and immediately turned to look at Nancy, who continued, "People here are always talking about this 'Black struggle,' but let's be real, you go to an expensive school with horses and shit that people back home could only dream of! It's always Black struggle this, Black struggle that, but how are you actually struggling at Madeira when everything is fucking given to you?" The spectators pounced on Nancy's rhetorical question before I could get a word in. "The *fuck*? What do *you* know about racism? You're white!" and "Just because you live with Black people doesn't mean shit" were some of the colorful comments said to put her in her place.

On the one hand, I felt like a fraud. The resources I enjoyed at Madeira were a privilege inaccessible to many. Who was I, as a sixteen-year-old prep student, to speak on the unique challenges facing Black people, especially when I was raised to not embrace my Black identity in America? On the other hand, I was aware that my access to resources was solely dependent on my academic performance. If I earned even one C, I was in jeopardy of losing my scholarship. I lived in a constant state of worry that the refuge Madeira was for me could also be easily stripped from me at a moment's notice. Poverty. That was my unspoken answer to Nancy's question. The Cooke Foundation and Madeira were underwriting my education now, but it wasn't a permanent fix to the poverty attached to me. That was my "big Black struggle."

I was trying to reconcile the conflicting perspectives while learning to hide my African identity to fit in somewhere. I sought solidarity with a set of Ghanaian twins in my cohort, but even they were uninterested in building sisterhood. They were pre-equipped with the knowledge that in white spaces like Madeira, race trumps ethnicity. Ideas about shared identity are first built on what people can see about you, not on what you tell them. Adopting a Black American identity was the path of least resistance for those who could play the part.

Visits from my mom were usually reserved for the days she picked me up for holiday breaks, but she'd occasionally make the forty-five-minute drive to surprise me with $20 for incidentals and Tupperware filled with Ghanaian food. On one visit she dropped off my favorite childhood dish: banku and fried blue-fish with lots of shito. Despite the buffet of options in the dining hall, nothing was as comforting as my mom's banku. I planned an entire event around the meal. I'd get through study hall that evening and make my way to the spacious and often empty common room in the dorm basement, where I could stretch out, heat up my food, and watch an episode of *Grey's Anatomy*. I was excited just thinking about it.

Hours passed and I was finally a few minutes into my plan. The episode was loaded, the fish was sizzling hot, and I was settled into a comfy beanbag chair when one of my Black classmates, Monica, entered the room. "What is *that*?" she asked, having never seen a ball of corn flour and cassava before or the pepper blend that covered the fish on my plate. I pointed to each item, defining them all while expecting her to ask for a bite—a customary practice among us boarding students who hunted for free food when the dining hall was closed. Instead, she turned her head and quickly placed her index finger under her nostrils. "It smells bad," she whispered just loud enough so I could hear but quiet enough so she didn't come off as rude to our white classmate on her laptop nearby. "Oh, sorry," I whispered back as I collected my things and left. I resigned myself to the storage room to eat my favorite meal among suitcases, having lost my appetite. The storage room became the safe space where I could eat the meals in secret my mom proudly prepared.

In the years to come, I made myself two promises as I embarked on college. The first was to pursue happiness. The weight of constantly masking my true identity to be palatable to others was crushing and discouraging. The second promise was to always have options and never make decisions based on desperation or financial hardship. I left high school with a boldness and appetite for risk taking because I'd been groomed to believe—for better or worse—that failure was *not* an option. There was no safety net on which to fall. I was my own best bet.

The Price on Happiness

Turns out, I was bamboozled into attending Boston College. From the student tour I had attended—which I later learned was specifically catered to students of color—BC seemed equal parts racially diverse and academically rigorous. But within days into my freshman year, I learned that the diversity I saw during my visit wasn't reality. In fact, I witnessed and experienced more acts of racism than inclusion from students and faculty alike. I knew I could tolerate this environment for the next four years, but the nagging question was if I wanted to, and would I be happy doing so? The answer was clear.

My first big risk was leaving the full-ride scholarship I had at Boston College to pursue a course of study and quality of life at NYU that better suited me. But another full ride wouldn't be waiting for me. I'd take on student debt that neither I nor my family had any foreseeable method to pay back. In telling my mom about my decision to leave Boston College her response was, "What do you mean you're not happy at Boston College? You're not paying anything. If you go to NYU, don't call me about money." That exchange set the tone for how I'd navigate the remainder of college and was a lesson in my mom's practice of capitalism, which required sacrificing happiness to avoid the risk of financial liability.

On my first day in the city, I unpacked my two suitcases and walked straight to NYU's Wasserman Center for Career Development to learn about work-study jobs and internships. I bought the skimpiest meal plan and hustled my way into a coveted library desk job in the middle of the school year.

Constantly on the hunt for ways to make money or save it, I found an in-house assistant job that allowed me to live rent free in the upscale Brooklyn Heights neighborhood, saving me thousands on room and board. The job proved to be a short-term sacrifice for a long-term gain. Ruth Rundell, the woman who hired me, was a kind, petite white woman with a blond bob. A journalist for a nationwide newspaper, she was often reading, traveling, or entertaining, and needed help caring for her teenage daughter, Cleo, and Snickers, their poodle-terrier mix. Living in the city had exposed me to the phenomenon of Black women nannying white children, but I'd never done it myself. The job was simple: Cook dinner for Cleo and myself on the evenings Ruth was out, and walk the dog twice a day. The money was good, and I appreciated their embrace of me and openness to having a stranger who didn't look like them live in their home.

My time with the Rundells gave me a sense of financial stability during college that I'd never yet had, but it came with a price. I became the scholar in residence on all race-related hot topics, carrying the burden of educating white people about their racial ignorance. I got used to working a lot and all the time. I juggled being the Rundell family assistant, a support worker at NYU's Bobst Library, and a teacher to underserved middle-school students in an academic-enrichment program, all while being a commuter student with a full course load and eyes set on graduating summa cum laude. The extra money I had at the end of each month I'd send home to help my mom cover utility bills. She never asked how I supported myself after my transfer to NYU, but she always thanked me for the money I sent. I took comfort in knowing that more than two decades since my birth, my mom was finally beginning to experience the return on investment of her many sacrifices.

The "Goldman Kool-Aid"

I made NYU's Career Center my second home during my last two years of college. I figured if staff members saw my face five days a week, they would remember me when opportunities came across their desks. Eventually my strategy paid off during my junior year. A staff member submitted my résumé to Goldman Sachs at the start of the firm's annual recruitment process to source junior talent. I wasn't attending NYU's Stern Business School or pursuing a degree in economics or finance. In fact, I knew nothing about high finance when I read the email inviting me to the firm's Sales and Trading Insight Day. But after one conversation with Dash, who had yet to formally start his career in the finance industry, he convinced me that this one-day event was the opportunity of a lifetime.

I spent the following summer interning at the firm's Environmental, Social, and Governance team, working long hours and learning in real time how to navigate the downside of hustle culture in corporate America. The culture shock was swift and unkind, but I stuck with it because I'd calculated that one summer of interning would allow me to wipe out 95 percent of my student debt—before my college graduation.

There was an air of competition within my small cohort that mirrored the culture of the place. We all wanted the return offer at the end of the summer and were well informed at the start of the internship that not everyone would receive one. This meant you had to overperform in your job function and outperform your peers. And on top of that, visibility was key. Raising your hand for extracurricular leadership roles, and strategically scheduling catch-ups with senior leadership to converse about your work deliverables and share your long-term professional goals at the firm kept you at the forefront when it was time for the recruiting committee to make final decisions.

But would all that labor be enough? Was merit truly the only thing that mattered in this so-called meritocratic system? I had naively believed in the myth of meritocracy at the start of college. But over time I learned the value of social networks and the power of shared racial identity with people in positions of influence. I was a rare Black face in a sea of whiteness. I'd learned that firms like Goldman Sachs had some success recruiting diverse talent but often struggled with retention. That made me wonder: Was I there on account of marketing optics, or were there people in positions of power somewhere who were invested in me for the long term? This experience was one of the many training grounds on which I learned what capitalism is and how it places demands on people according to who they are. My disciplined upbringing—relentlessly focused on hard work, excellence, and determination—wasn't enough in comparison to my mostly white male colleagues with whom I struggled to relate. My Black identity shaped—and continues to shape—my engagement with capitalism because it requires a heightened level of strategic and futuristic thinking, emotional and relational awareness, and the discernment to dismiss certain problematic cultural norms in service of the greater goal—financial freedom and a life full of options.

Being a Black participant of capitalism is entirely different from being a white participant and demands a different set of requirements. This unequal distinction was created by capitalism itself. Black people are promoted more slowly, and Black women, especially, get paid less on the dollar than white men. For many of us, we hustle because we are, quite literally, being shortchanged. Black people's engagement with capitalism requires a deep awareness of the system that ensnares you. It requires that we always stay vigilant, and it is in this vigilance that we can change the systems we are given.

Not one day passed in my ten-week internship when I did not feel anxious and sick to my stomach at the thought of not receiving a return offer—what I considered failure in my shot at escaping a life of scraping by and the life my mother had found a challenge to raise us in. A large part of my chronic anxiety came from my struggle to reconcile the altruistic nature of my environmental and social impact work with the core mandate of the firm: Make money while simultaneously finding ways to save it.

My team built social impact programs with a focus on advancing racial diversity to increase the firm's influence, presence, and investment in local communities. But a question I always received was, "Why are we doing this?" Understandably—albeit still frustrating—"It's the right thing to do" was not the correct answer. Instead, something to the effect of "reputational risk management" (which really meant taking action to limit the release of bad press about the firm) would temporarily satisfy senior leaders until the next ask for a budget to build out another program.

My colleagues would joke about how I didn't do "real work" because it was viewed as people-oriented "charity work" and didn't rely on extensive spreadsheets, datasets, and dashboards of visual analytics. I'd laugh along but knew they meant what they said. Between my need to justify that the work I did was, in fact, work and my need to do the extra labor of persuading leadership of its value proposition, I constantly worried that I was falling short. So I'd come home to more work.

Most of the people I worked closely with on efforts to reduce the firm's environmental impact sat in the firm's Bengaluru office—roughly eleven hours ahead of Eastern Standard Time. As the intern working alongside full-time employees, I adjusted to their schedules. And so after attending one of the many required networking happy hours as the nondrinker that I am, I'd hurry home to cook dinner for Cleo and feed and walk Snickers before logging back in to work to talk about carbon reduction tracking with the team for an hour or two. All the while, my work with the Rundells was a reminder of how, at one time in history, Black women's participation in capitalism was limited to domestic work.

I still remember receiving the offer as if it happened this morning. It was late August, a few weeks before the start of the semester, and I was already at my NYU work-study job at the Avery Fisher Media Center when I got a call from an undisclosed 212 number. I knew immediately it was the recruiter and hurried out of the center to find a quiet place I could either celebrate or cry. "Hello, this is Rachel," I said in the most professional, even-keeled voice I could muster. Caroline the recruiter and I exchanged a few pleasantries until a pregnant pause settled between us, which I knew would be followed by the reason for her call. I didn't realize I had stopped breathing until I took a quick exhale once she said, "Congratulations, I'd like to extend you a full-time offer."

That was the precise moment I felt I had "gotten out." All the sacrifice, anxiety, and stress of juggling so much felt worth it, and there was a peacefulness that came with this promise of economic security. But despite "getting out," the anxiety of "falling back" has stayed with me. This, too, is Black Capitalism.

What was the underlying desire that evoked such an emotional response in me over the course of a five-minute call? And who was the emotion for? It wasn't the full-time offer in and of itself that I really wanted—it was the freedom that came with it not only for myself but also for my family. The exhale I took after receiving the news wasn't just for that moment. It was a release from years of holding my breath hoping that my hustle and grind would produce a return on investment whereby both I and my loved ones could get free. I could breathe easier now knowing that the pressure on my mom to sustain herself was no longer a concern. I now had access to the resources to make her American Dream a reality.

Sharing the news with Mom and Dash came as a relief to them too. Dash's first words were "You're golden, pun intended," because the exclusive Goldman Sachs stamp of approval on my résumé had the power to alter the trajectory of my entire professional career. My mom, completely unaware of what Goldman Sachs is and the particulars of the financial industry, was just happy that in a time where college students were, and still are, graduating with debilitating student loans and poor job prospects, I was debt free and employed—making more money as a twenty-two-year-old than she's made in her lifetime.

Being happy about receiving a full-time offer was not about liking capitalism or not—that's beside the point. To get and stay free, strategically engaging with capitalism allowed me to believe that just maybe the future could be different for us. I came back to school my senior year lighter, knowing that I'd graduate without the burden of debt weighing on my shoulders.

After graduation, I would go back to the firm full-time with a better sense of what to expect. But knowing the culture of competition, working to exhaustion, handling microaggressions, and scheming for visibility from leadership wouldn't make the daily grind any easier for me. I knew the culture wasn't a good personality fit, but my reprieve was in my mission: Stay for a while, collect a check, then go produce knowledge and teach about race and money in academia with a full piggy bank.

The Undercommons of Wall Street

The general term *Black Capitalism*, not as I re-create it anew in this book, dates back to post–World War II. It had been sold to Black people in different ways for decades as we've tried to achieve its promise of wealth through varied means. The food and beverage franchise industry, civil service, government, and even healthcare are some of the professional routes that have been marketed to Black people. In the mid- to late twentieth century, following the assassination of Martin Luther King Jr., federal programs led by Presidents Johnson and Nixon to address racial injustice promoted the idea that the quality of Black life could advance through Black proprietary ownership of businesses. The franchise industry is one case study. Political pundits of the time believed that if Black people owned fast-food establishments, like McDonald's, in their own neighborhoods, then their economic power would increase.[1] This prompted a collaboration between fast-food companies, Black businesspeople, and civil rights leaders to test the theory.[2] As a result, Black ownership of fast-food companies skyrocketed, as did Black wealth.[3] Prince Akeem's (Eddie Murphy's character) employment at "McDowell's" in the 1988 film Coming to America was not just comedic, but a sign of the times.

The healthcare industry is another advertised path to Black wealth that the children of African immigrants know especially well. "Go into nursing—it's secure and the pay is good" is an instruction many of my Ghanaian friends gripe about hearing from their parents, and yet follow because of the allure of financial security. It strikes me that these institutional pathways include covert physical spaces that Stefano Harney and Fred Moten describe in their book The Undercommons. Harney and Moten define "the undercommons" as a subversive space where marginalized groups with shared objectives form a community within an institution or industry.[4] I discovered their book soon after I started full-time at Goldman Sachs, and it forever altered the way I thought about how people can relate to their workplace.

According to Harney and Moten, the undercommons is a safe space where people can call out the failings of an organization, and its inability to fully realize corporate ideals because of its flaws, while acting upon the resources it has to provide.[5] Members of the undercommons do not naively seek out or expect corporate inclusion because they are aware of the systemic harms the institutional body produces, including racism. Instead, group members engage in what Harney and Moten call "fugitive planning"—the practice of discovering new ways to exist beyond the grip of institutional power to evade "capture."[6] If this concept seems abstract, consider the creation of the Underground Railroad during the institution of slavery in the United States as one concrete example of fugitive planning in action. As people—enslaved and free—realized that they could not upend the system, they created an undercommons within it—the Underground Railroad—where activists became conductors and carried out the work of fugitive planning to liberate themselves and one another. The undercommons is one of the few, if not only, places of refuge for marginalized groups within social structures of inequity.

The university (historically Black colleges and universities are another site for the undercommons) within a predominantly white academia is the context for the authors' argument. But I wondered if their ideas would apply to the finance industry, or any place of work? Who makes up the firm's undercommons that exploit the firm's resources despite its unachieved mission to advance sustainable diverse and inclusive business practices? Are these subversive professionals the same ones who are perceived as "diverse" professionals? And do they look to the firm, and their place within it, as a pathway to financial stability?

These questions swirled in my mind as I made myself the subject of inquiry. Was I behaving subversively because of my intention to exploit the firm's resources to serve my own needs? Some might have called me a diversity hire, but was I using that to my benefit? Church and school were outlets in my past—was the undercommons of Goldman Sachs my new haven? The answer to these questions was yes. And over time, I realized I wasn't the only one making trade-offs while learning and developing the strategies needed to thrive on Wall Street and beyond. For the purposes of this book, the undercommons is the discrete communal space Black people create on Wall Street and in the financial industry writ large. And the practice of Black Capitalism on Wall Street and beyond is one unique form of fugitive planning to resist and challenge inequitable institutional power.

Together we make up the undercommons: a community of Black professionals who are conscious of their marginal status and work together to share resources, build social networks, and develop the tactics needed to combat institutional racism.

I found refuge in the undercommons. Many of the people I met and had conversations with about race, class, and Goldman Sachs's work culture became friends. We worked together, confided in one another, and supported one another in creating a workplace where we could succeed. I'd ultimately leave Goldman Sachs to pursue my doctorate at Yale, but I eventually returned to the undercommons of Wall Street to research how it is a space to both see and understand Black Capitalist thriving in action.

And what I learned challenged the overly simplified portrayals of Black financiers we so often see displayed in popular culture, including television shows about money, wealth, and greed. One series that interests me is the Showtime hit *Billions*.

Though marketed to a white audience, it offers more racial diversity than comparable shows, with a whopping four Black characters in its first few seasons. It's with this "saturation" of Blackness that the politics and absurdity of Black representation come into view. The demographics of the hedge fund that the story plot is built around mirrors the demographics of the American financial industry—a lot of middle-aged white men. The three non-male white employees are each tokenized. One is the female caretaker of the firm's employees. The second is the employee hungry for self-validation, burdened to prove her worth among her male counterparts. And the third is the unusually brilliant gender-nonconforming employee who is respected for their smarts but intentionally referred to as "her" instead of "they" by colleagues.

Meanwhile, the four "main" Black characters hold a marginal status at the firm and in the show's plotline. One is perceived as cold, stoic, and uninterested in enmeshing herself within the culture of the firm. The second is exploited for his cultural expertise yet positioned as inconsequential to the firm despite his invaluable contribution during a moment of financial instability. The third is propped up as a socialite whose tangible skills take second fiddle to her physical appeal. Meanwhile, the fourth Black character is mysterious, methodical, and ambitious. Portrayed as an opportunist, this character strategically positions herself to acquire as much power as possible in the imminent wreckage.

In drama-packed seasons portraying Wall Street's most elite power players, Black representation looks like a hostile woman who is isolated and ignored, an analyst who keeps his head down and gets by through assimilating, the sexy and alluring love interest, and the career-driven professional who is detached from her own humanity. These stereotypes fail to capture the breadth and depth of Black people's lived experiences within the financial industry. And yet they resemble the troubling ways Black Capitalists are often labeled by their white counterparts in real life. It's important to bear in mind that any effort to collapse racial stereotypes creates a problematic possibility—swapping one set of racialized stereotypes for its opposite.

Representation is a funny thing. I remember being in my African American studies theory course and reading the work of Stuart Hall. Born in Jamaica in 1932, Hall was a British Marxist sociologist, cultural theorist, and political activist. I had just watched a documentary about race in America through the lens of O. J. Simpson and his pursuit of a non-Black identity (remember his famous line "I'm not Black, I'm O.J."), which brought to life for me Hall's theories about identity politics.[7] Hall argues in his seminal book *Representation: Cultural Representations and Signifying Practices,* "Escaping the grip of one stereotypical extreme (blacks are poor, childish, subservient, always shown as servants, everlastingly 'good,' in menial positions, deferential to whites, never the heroes, . . .) may simply mean being trapped in its stereotypical 'other' (blacks are motivated by money, [and] love bossing white people around . . .)."[8]

So, how then do the real-life experiences of those in the undercommons extend our understanding of how Black people negotiate their relationship to reductive stereotypes like the ones portrayed in *Billions,* and what it means to be Black on Wall Street? Turns out, Hall's theory holds up in the lives of Black professionals I talked to who said, "I want race to be the footnote of my career." Unlike Simpson, these Black professionals are *not* saying that they don't want to be Black. It's not that their Black identity doesn't matter to them. What they *are* saying is that they don't want to be defined by the racism that Black people have to overcome since society only understands Blackness through the racism that it puts on us. In the following chapters I tell the tales of five Black Capitalists who are members of the undercommons. Their chosen and diverse paths of cultural assimilation, subversive resistance, and the in-between in crucial moments such as corporate America's moral reckoning in the wake of George Floyd's murder uncover the strategies and tactics Black people have learned in order to successfully participate in capitalism as Black professionals.

Their stories are part of a collection of interviews I conducted with over two hundred people. Though I talked to both men and women, the five stories included here are of Black men. In fact, most of my interviews were with men, which speaks to the demographics of the financial industry. What I learned from the women I spoke to is that they share the universal plight of Black women in any industry, but especially one dominated by white men. Black women are often underpaid and confront multiple forms of bias across gender, race, and ethnicity. The financial industry, as we'll see in the popularized shows I'll discuss, is an environment where Black women especially must be strategic and careful in what they share and with whom. The Black men who spoke to me generally understood that their gender would shield them in the same way these Black women understood their gender would not.

As an anthropologist and a Black woman, I share with these women the feeling and fact of precarity. They were wary of who they could trust because racism and sexism in the industry isolate people—Black women in particular. More than any other group, Black women are fiercely punished for their confidence. They cannot work hard enough to work themselves into protection. The better our work, the more precarious our status. To give voice to the experiences they've endured is to be perceived as the "angry Black woman" who is "irrational," "difficult," and "uncooperative." The common practice of calling Black women angry, especially when they are telling the truth, is a tactical strategy employed to invalidate their humanity and undercut their credibility. The added danger of this label is that people, in an act of self-preservation and faulty allyship, are quick to disassociate from Black women who are regarded as a problem to those with institutional power. This practice of social isolation in the workplace jeopardizes the professional outcomes of Black women and makes the price of disclosure too great to bear.

To protect the privacy of people in a society that punishes victims rather than the guilty, I use my own story as a stand-in and call attention to this choice since there is no such thing as an objective observer. The experiences of the Black women I spoke to are experiences I also share. I realized we were all telling the same story. But the only person I will put in harm's way is me when even anonymity cannot promise the feeling of safety for Black women. This choice is unconventional for many anthropologists. But anthropology as a discipline is a traditionally white Western pursuit in need of reconstruction. In the same way I draw connection between Blackness and capitalism, I also acknowledge that anthropology has been traditionally racist. My decision to protect the Black women who spoke with me is one example of solidarity and community-making in anthropology.

CHAPTER 2

The Spook Who Sat by the Door

I ran to catch the B26 bus I saw speeding down the street toward downtown Brooklyn. My destination was Alex's Full Moon gathering. Although we had worked in different divisions, Alex and I first met at Goldman Sachs during a Black History Month event. Our friendship started then and grew after my departure from the firm as he allowed me access into his personal life in part to pursue my research.

Central to Alex's Black American identity was his practice of traditional West African spirituality as an Ifa priest. I was eager to attend the gathering to learn about what Alex described as how to "connect to the spirits." Alex greeted me at the door with a sympathetic smile that was his polite way of commenting on my unnecessary punctuality. He introduced me to the three others in the industrial-style apartment. They were rolling blunts and cooking jerk chicken, coconut rice, and chickpea curry stew. As guests started trickling in, Alex invited them to take a "light bath": dipping their hands in a concoction of water, sand, and pieces of jade plant to sprinkle onto their shoulders and heads. This practice of the Akan people from Ghana was a cleansing ritual to prepare to connect with the deities. He'd then lead us in another, more intricate bathing ritual that spiritually opened us to hear the voice of our ancestors and receive messages, gifts, and guidance.

All of Alex's guests were people of color, predominantly queer Black men, most of whom practiced African Traditional Religion (ATR) or another form of spirituality: witchcraft, astrology, numerology, and Ifa among others. Alex expressed his intent for the evening: to create a safe space for queer people of color to gather to engage in and learn about ATR. With that, the ceremony began. At the altar of a deity shrine Alex poured water and gin as an offering to the deities while reciting Yoruba prayers. The prayers were made to break through the earth and declare one's desire to create a portal to the deities.

As Alex repeated the prayers in English, he invited us to say the names of our ancestors and requested that the deities watch over and empower us with strength, wisdom, and discernment. A soft buzz filled the room as guests whispered the names of their family members who had transitioned into the next life.

Following the libation, Alex left the room to seek spiritual consultation with an outdoor shrine for the travel deity Esu, which Alex had received from Nigeria during his priesthood initiation the year before. He prayed that Esu would protect us by tricking our enemies and blocking negativity from entering our homes. Using obikola and orogbo nuts to carry out the divination, Alex tapped each of our heads with the nuts to include us in the prayer, repeatedly casting the nuts on the floor until the configuration on the concrete signaled that our prayers had been accepted. This concluded the formal rites, and Alex invited us to share our own spiritual journeys. I learned what it was like to practice Ifa from the perspective of a sixty-year-old gay Puerto Rican man. Black men spoke on how their queer identities marked their turn away from Western religious practice and toward alternate spiritual beliefs free of sexism and homophobia. We laughed, danced, told stories, and read tarot cards late into the night.

Alex's Full Moon gathering left me curious about how his personal life influences his work life as a Goldman Sachs employee. Over coffee a few weeks after the event, he shared his perspective with me. "Africans are struggling in this place, it's not for us, but this place is a means," he reflected. He added that he thinks of himself as a "spy"—gaining access, acquiring excess resources and money, and funneling it back to his Black communities in Brooklyn. "I'm going in, getting this experience, getting this knowledge and taking it to my community and applying it," he said with conviction. One example of how he's been able to do this is the employee-led volunteer day he organized to funnel human capital support and firm money to his dance company, Asha. The visibility created a snowball effect that resulted in more than $1,000 raised in ticket sales among Goldman Sachs employees for Asha's upcoming dance concert. Alex's access to Black people with money to spend made it possible for the firm to support Asha in an impactful way.

The situational awareness Alex has developed because of his intentional choice to be a spy is the difference between assimilation and code-switching for him. Acting as a liaison between his predominantly white workspace and his Black community, he's morphed his speaking habits so that the way he talks is "digestible" to white people without entailing assimilation to white culture. "I'm an envoy in this foreign space," he told me. "I've trained, I've watched white people, I know how they work and operate. And what they don't think I know is that I know myself. That's what makes it powerful. They don't think I know myself; they think I'm assimilated; they think I'm one of them. Meanwhile, I know exactly who I am."

The tension at play is Alex's belief that Goldman Sachs is not designed for Black people to thrive despite the access to resources the firm can provide his community. Adopting a covert demeanor and strategy reconciles the conflict and empowers Alex to be purposefully *in* but not *of* the firm. To successfully navigate Goldman Sachs, and Wall Street by extension, one must understand the firm's politics and cultural practices, deliver exceptional business results, and climb the corporate ladder through strategic networking. Alex does this to subvert the assimilation process embedded in these activities. He is perceived as an ideal "diversity hire" due to his networking skills, work product, and popularity among colleagues. The firm capitalizes on his racial identity and publicly disclosed sexual orientation. But unbeknown to Goldman Sachs, Alex masks his rogue and subversive behavior in what the firm considers a model culture carrier committed to advancing the longevity of the firm.

The Spectrum from Assimilation to Resistance

Alex's choice to be a spy, channeling previously inaccessible resources and information to his community, is just one of the many actions people take to fill equity gaps both within and outside the workplace. Some invest their time in diversity recruiting initiatives to increase the recruitment and retention of Black professionals at the firm. Many of those I interviewed disapprove of how their firms manage diversity recruiting, noting that it's a job "usually held by white women who are out of touch" with the population they're targeting. Additionally, seasoned Black professionals are often compelled to take on the responsibility of mentoring junior Black talent due to the gaps in representation of Black professionals at the senior level who can inspire retention. It's part of the invisible and uncompensated work of reconstructing the racial landscape of the finance industry to create more opportunities for Black Capitalist thriving to exist.

Others volunteer for leadership roles in business resource groups to create firm strategies that specifically support the professional development of underrepresented professionals. Some of the institutional power Black business leaders have accumulated during their time at the firm is used to develop the Black professional population. These activities and behaviors reveal just some of the community-oriented work led by Black Capitalists on Wall Street.

The challenging work to advance equity from within the industry is but one feature of Black people's lived experience. There's a tax applied to just being a Black person on Wall Street—never mind lifting as you climb. For Black people on Wall Street, choosing to assimilate without subversive or ulterior motives is a useful strategy to simply get through the workday, because to show up in spaces maintained by structural racism *is political,* whether we want it to be or not. But what is resistance?

Surprisingly, one of the few places that I've most accurately seen the politics of Black Capitalism and its ethical contradictions on display is in the satirical niche Showtime series *Black Monday,* starring Don Cheadle. It tracks the life of an outrageous, power-hungry Black broker who owns a small-scale yet well-respected investment firm in the 1980s. But as it turns out, the broker has a big secret that haunts him: his past life as a Black Panther Party member. The character's politics err on the side of civil disobedience rather than radicalized and strategic violent disobedience. So it's depicted as strange that a man invested in the philosophies of the Black Panther Party could turn into a staunch proponent of American capitalism. The two political identities are in opposition—or so it seems. This fictive portrayal represents the real ultimatum often presented to Black people.

A Black person is either radical in their reimagination of the political economy but disengaged from it or active in capitalism but not radical in their transformation of it. One must choose either a life of protest and resistance to systems that engender inequality or a life of comfort and access bankrolled by the tools of capitalism. The ultimatum suggests the two identities cannot coexist within a person. The moral implications are clear: Either sacrifice one's life for the higher cause of Black liberation or sell one's soul to capitalism and become an agent of the economic devastation it so often produces.

The ultimatum is one I've personally grappled with. I'm a business owner and work in the financial industry known for its long and current history of exploiting Black people. And yet I was raised in a Black, radical politics. According to this, what choice have I picked? The point is that the ultimatum, a set of false choices, begs the question: Is it possible to thrive in capitalism while remaining sensitive and responsive to the harms of capitalism? The answer is yes. But an awareness of the racialized inequality capitalism produces, coupled with a resolve to transform the political economy through one's engagement *in* it, is what makes the dual identity difficult for many to imagine. *Black Monday,* like many of us, falls prey to the limited imagination that capitalism hopes we have. But to live as a Black Capitalist is to live in the imagination of what has not *yet* been done.

To Be a (Black) Man on Wall Street

W. E. B. Du Bois, who coined the phrase *double consciousness,* and Frantz Fanon, the author of *Black Skin, White Masks,* were prominent Black scholars of their time who created useful theories about how Black men can reclaim their humanity after being denied it through Western colonialism and slavery. Born in 1868 and the first Black man to earn a doctorate from Harvard University, Du Bois believed that a Black man's pursuit of higher education is the way to achieve a distinguished life and to peacefully exist in a multiracial society. Born in Martinique in 1925 and educated as a psychiatrist in France, Fanon had a different approach. He believed that no matter the amount of education a Black man obtains, it will only allow him to better resemble a white man, but never unlock the freedom to be perceived as a man. Fanon's solution to this problem was self-invention: making the active choice to decide for yourself who you are without concern for the white gaze or the history of slavery and colonialism imposed on Black people. Du Bois's and Fanon's theories are distinct yet can coexist, and they do so in the everyday lives of Black people. Their ideas from decades past, which are lived out in the present, uncover the tax on Blackness and the specific challenges Black people encounter in the fight to be recognized for their humanity.

In *The Souls of Black Folk,* Du Bois contends that Black men hold three dominant beliefs about their humanity dating back to American slavery. The first is a desire to meet one's basic human needs, with the understanding that it takes cooperation (coerced or otherwise) to do so.[1] Sustaining oneself cannot be done in isolation. And, because these human needs cut across racial groups, pursuing them in community with one another can inspire human unity.[2] The second thought, a vestige of the antebellum South, is "the sincere and passionate belief that somewhere between men and cattle, God created a *tertium quid,* and called it a Negro—a clownish, simple creature, at times even lovable within its limitations, but straitly foreordained to walk within the Veil."[3] Buried deep within this belief is a lack of self-worth first planted by white people who fear what could happen if the Black man acted in defense of his humanity. The idea that a Black person is a *tertium quid*—a "third thing," neither human nor animal—coupled with the constant threat of death by lynching, keeps the Black man where the white man has put him and preserves the social architecture of white supremacy.[4]

Du Bois claims that the Black man learned the first two thoughts from the white man and, as a result, came to the third one on his own. The desire for liberty, freedom, and opportunity is couched in his self-doubt. The Black man asks himself: "Suppose, after all, the World is right and we are less than men? Suppose this mad impulse within is all wrong, some mock mirage from the untrue?"[5] Du Bois's concern is the way Black men question their humanity because of this internalized thinking. Thoughts of human unity, the forced inferiority of Black men, and the cries for freedom made by men who are not sure if freedom is their birthright are all at war in the Black man's mind.[6]

Du Bois proposes a new way forward to combat the plight of Black America: "The foundations of knowledge in this race, as in others, must be sunk deep in the college and university if we would build a solid, permanent structure."[7] Du Bois believes that the social advancement of Black people could only be achieved through "study and thought and an appeal to the rich experiences of the past."[8] The higher education of the Black man is the admission ticket to a dignified life. Though racial tensions would continue to persist (as Du Bois accurately foretold the phenomenon of colorism in the twentieth century and beyond), education had the wherewithal to produce human unity. Or so he thought.

Writing *Black Skin, White Masks* nearly fifty years after the publication of *The Souls of Black Folk,* Frantz Fanon details a sobering account of race relations during Martiniquan colonialism. Opposing Du Bois's assertion that higher education can allow the Black man to realize his full humanity, Fanon contends that the education of a Black man will make him "proportionately whiter—that is, he will come closer to being a real human being."[9] Education does not grant a Black man the privilege to just be, but rather the understanding of how to adopt the behaviors of white people. One learns how to perform whiteness in order to resemble, but never reach, humanity.

Witnessing the psychological toll of colonialism on Black men, Fanon draws the "painful" conclusion that "for the black man there is only one destiny. And it is white."[10] Holding these feelings of inadequacy, the Black man lives in a society that says "sin is Negro as virtue is white"—he is guilty and, while not knowing of what, he is no good.[11]

Fanon argues that many Black men accept this destiny and concede "the unarguable superiority of the white man."[12] But Fanon does not. He rejects the past as an indication for what is in store for his destiny.[13] Yearning for better, he cries, "I do not have the right to allow myself to bog down. I do not have the right to allow the slightest fragment to remain in my existence. I do not have the right to allow myself to be mired in what the past has determined. I am not the slave of the Slavery that dehumanized my ancestors."[14] Fanon's resolve to *just be* first begins with the self-reminder "that the real leap consists in introducing invention into existence."[15] Fanon wills his freedom into existence by robbing history of its power over his psyche and self-expression. He invents himself by writing a new history that starts with his present.

On the one hand, Du Bois's theory offers higher education as a way to navigate and excel *within* rigid racial categories. On the other hand, Fanon tenders a psychological theory that points Black people toward an entirely different kind of education—self-invention. Du Bois and Fanon seem to be at odds, but neither theory is mutually exclusive. The ideas of both scholars are compatible with each other and are evident in the lived experiences of many Black professionals today.

◆ ◆ ◆

Chris, a Nigerian American corporate tax specialist, embodies the conflicts and desires of Black people that Du Bois and Fanon theorize decades ago. His dream to *just be* shapes his expression of Black masculinity in the workplace, as an analyst at Goldman Sachs and as an associate at JPMorganChase, and now in his current role as a vice president at Morgan Stanley. Chris's story reveals another way race makes a difference in how we participate in capitalism, the methods employed to merely exist in racially charged spaces, and the cost of doing so.

Chris grew up on the west side of under-resourced Detroit, which came with its fair share of challenges. Having lost his father in the seventh grade, he recalls middle school as "one of the toughest times" of his life. His school "underserved a group of people that deserved a lot more attention," he says, and he credits his mom for keeping him focused on education while he watched others embark on different paths. Chris tested into Renaissance High School, where 99 percent of graduates matriculate into four-year institutions, making Chris's trajectory almost inevitable. As a Math Core scholarship recipient, he attended Wayne State University's business school, where his passion for numbers and quantitative analysis flourished. By the end of his sophomore year he declared a major in accounting and went on to complete six internships by the end of his undergraduate studies. A fellowship with the nonprofit organization Sponsors for Educational Opportunity landed him a tax internship at Goldman Sachs, which was his entry into the world of investment banking.

Chris has now spent years in the financial services industry, all of which were fraught with racial tension. As we chatted, I was curious to learn how his Black identity either challenged or supported the message of meritocracy championed by leaders at his current and former firms. "You want your work product to be all that people judge you on, but it's not. It's not that simple," he recounted. Though many people believe that they are inclusive, they hold known or unknown biases. The reality of that has made him hyperaware of his Blackness. He is the only Black male in his department, and there are times when he feels his race makes him stand out more among his colleagues. Reflecting on the early days of his career, he recalled, "I felt like I was in it alone because the people that were there to comfort me were Black but not in tax or were in tax but weren't Black. But as I've gotten further in my career, I tend to block it out but it's still there."

I pressed him to share why he avoids thinking about his

Black identity at work. "When I was harping on being racially alone on this journey, it was just depressing. I felt a sense of hopelessness. I always felt like I was looking over my shoulder at department functions and that I couldn't talk to certain people. I also felt a sense of representation. I felt proud, too, but I had to learn how to be proud," he said. But Chris also realized that before him, there was no one else like him, and that made him proud. However, he would still try to prevent himself from thinking about race because he worried it would distract him from obtaining his goals. "I had to re-channel my energy and focus on things that were going to allow me to be the best and most productive in that moment," he explained. "When you harp on that isolation, you tend to lose focus and have a victim mentality. I didn't want to be the underdog even though most would say that I am."

As I've gotten to know Chris over the years, I've seen how his appreciation for higher education, rational thinking, and analysis has benefited him professionally. I've also witnessed the evolution of his thinking on race. Recent conversations show his interest in the collective human race rather than any one race, and he self-identifies as melanated rather than Black in a personal attempt to challenge the social construction of race itself. Chris's consciousness of the stereotypes attributed to Black men informs how he expresses his masculinity. He strives to be an authentic version of himself at work but careful to appear non-threatening to his white colleagues.

And yet the firm champions a meritocratic culture aimed to democratize the opportunity of professional advancement for all employees. Employees are told that their work product is what matters. The discrepancy between Chris's experience and the firm's cultural narrative is indicative of a corporate phenomenon that leaves many Black professionals wanting to be judged by the content of their work product rather than the color of their skin. The confrontation between Chris's intimate desires to be an unrestrained self-made man and the fixed sociocultural norms of the financial industry show just how inescapable Blackness can be and the difference it makes in one's professional experience.

Fanon's embodied theory to "be a man and nothing but a man" resonates with Chris's desire to just be. The underlying hope in Fanon's declaration is the chance to define himself without the comparison to whiteness. Chris can freely express himself at work if his self-expression meets the expectations of his white colleagues, the firm benefits from his racial diversity, and his work product is not hindered by the intersection of his racial and gender difference. He works within these constraints while striving to maintain distance from them.

Obtaining the higher education needed to work in the elite world of high finance does not ensure that one won't be reduced to or viewed through one's Black identity. And despite individual action taken to downplay racial difference, firms still target and highlight the racial diversity of Black employees for commercial gain. The mental and physical labor required to account for one's Blackness in predominantly white spaces that exploit the racial diversity of their employees can feel like a catch-22. Wall Street is in a conflicting entanglement with post-racial meritocratic rhetoric and its dependency on the racial diversity of some employees to market itself as a great place to work for Black professionals. The point is not the range of feelings and behaviors Black people have in response to how their racial identity is perceived by colleagues. It's the fact that one's Black identity must be considered and subsequently managed when adjusting to the norms of Wall Street to succeed in the industry—a mental calibration Wall Street's majority does not have to do. They enjoy the freedom to *just be*.

What added demands are placed exclusively on Black people when nationwide racial uproar with global reach incites Wall Street, and corporate America by extension, to action? In the following sections I chronicle the personal and collective accounts of Black professionals presented with a difficult choice: opt in or out of corporate America's moral reckoning.

To Be *In* but Not *Of*?

Shortly after the police killing of George Floyd on May 25, 2020, Dave, the CEO of a multibillion-dollar asset advisory firm, reached out to me for help navigating conversations about race and racism in the workplace. He was eager to address what he called "blind spots" in his thinking about diversity and inclusion. He recalled scrolling through his list of LinkedIn contacts, searching for someone who might be able to recommend meaningful action to take at his firm to adequately cultivate a culture of racial diversity and inclusion. The only person who fit the bill was me.

I found my singularity odd not because I questioned if Dave had *any* colleagues who raised questions of race to him previously, but rather because of Dave's own identity as a Southeast Asian man. "Doesn't he know a thing or two about racism?" I wondered to myself. He shared stories with me at the start of our meeting about moments of exclusion he had encountered at the start of his professional career that did not square with his present desire to understand marginalization as a corporate phenomenon (as if it were a foreign concept he had never grappled with before).

Sensing my confusion, he shared how the demands of his advisory firm at its onset created gaps he now attempts to fill. At its start, Dave's company was composed of all men, the majority of whom were Indian in the white-male-dominated world of high finance. He believed that to be effectively commercial, his team needed to visibly reflect his white-male clientele and thus began the process of building a workforce to mirror racialized and cultural aspects of the financial industry rather than disrupt it. Dave was familiar with navigating finance and whiteness, but for all his successes in that domain, he still found himself falling short when it came to understanding the complexity of race and racism in the workplace and the problematic norms professionals of color can feel compelled to abide by.

On our Zoom call I found myself summarizing some of the findings of my own research and that of others. I and other social scientists have found that senior leaders use the rhetoric of culture to instill collective modes of behavior and thinking across the workforce to produce effective professional communities. Historian Kathryn Lofton contends that corporate culture is shaped by "how individual leaders foster visionary accounts of an organization's values, and then develop reward systems and rituals to teach, inculcate, and reiterate these values."[16] In effect, workplace cultures "establish identifiable moods and motivations" that become deeply internalized by employees who in turn commit themselves to an organization's values, structure, and order of things to maintain the perception of an ideal corporate culture regardless of whether the ideal is reality. The reward systems and rituals that reaffirm corporate values create a powerful state of delusion and denial about the gap between the corporation's values and its actual culture.

Everyday workplace behaviors created by corporate cultural norms are antithetical to the creation of inclusive workplaces. As seen in conversations on race, racism, and police brutality in workplaces nationwide, leaders are being asked to listen and act in ways that support the most marginalized communities—the undercommons—within their organizations. While many financial firms on Wall Street have committed significant charitable dollars to external organizations that aim to support Black communities, Black professionals are still left wondering, if not outright asking, "What is being done internally and by whom to change the culture of where I work?"

After we spoke, Dave recommended that I meet with members of his team, including Helen, his chief marketing officer. The greatest takeaway from my conversation with Helen was insight into how corporate responses to racism are constructed, if at all, by the most senior voices of the firm. As she noted: "There is some level of uncertainty because there currently is not one Black voice to turn to on my team or in the firm in order to better understand the situation [or] to speak adequately on it." In this case, we see how the absence of a Black professional in the organization can become justification for white senior leadership to choose silence rather than action. In effect, a lack of racial diversity is the alibi for their ignorance.

A week following my conversation with Helen, I attended an intimate social gathering hosted by my friend Allan, an Ethiopian executive director in sales and trading at JPMorganChase. The professional experience of the attendees ranged from finance, housing and infrastructure development, consulting, and the nonprofit sector. While eating Senegalese food with Afrobeats playing in the background, we talked about the nation's current moral reckoning with its long-standing living history of racism and what we, as well as our varied employers, are and are not doing to address it. "What do y'all think about what's going on right now?" someone asked the group. "It's sad to say but honestly, I'm not surprised by any of it. Have they ever stopped killing us? It's just fucked up that I'm numb to it," another replied. The silent nods of agreement by others in the room proved that they weren't alone.

Allan spoke about writing a letter via email to senior leadership about the necessity of action. Another attendee recalled a conversation she had with her white CEO in which she challenged him to do more than provide his usual lip service. Another attendee bemoaned the well-intended yet problematic actions of her white female colleague. And another talked about having to usurp the position of diversity and inclusion facilitator haphazardly taken up by one of his white female colleagues whose actions "only made things worse," as he put it.

Thinking back to my conversation with Helen, I asked if it is our responsibility as Black professionals to buy into or opt out of leadership roles in corporate America's moral reckoning on race and racism. The infrastructure strategist laid out the pros and cons of both positions. Opting into and spearheading corporate reform clearly benefits the organization to the extent that senior leadership listens and responds to the recommendations provided by Black professionals. Opting out can ensure an individual's sense of sanity by avoiding the burden of having to repeatedly educate one's colleagues and the possibility that such teachable moments can fall on deaf ears. At best, opting out can redirect accountability and responsibility onto white senior leadership to act; at worst, it can silently reaffirm and approve of the status quo.

The consultant in the room, who disclosed being rather senior in his organization, argued that it is our responsibility as Black professionals to lead the discourse, especially if we are in positions of high visibility and power. Allan nodded in agreement and added the caveat that while the circumstances are unfortunate and that buy-in or opt-out ultimately should be one's choice, we as Black professionals cannot stay silent and this is the time to be bold in our asks to firms across industries.

My research shows that the ambivalent position Black professionals have in terms of buying in or opting out is nothing new but part and parcel of long-standing Black professional engagement within corporate America. However, something about this sociopolitical moment of collective protest *does* feel new and indicative of higher stakes. I asked several Black professionals, and the common denominator was the flagrancy of George Floyd's murder coupled with the watchful eye of corporate stakeholders. They also mentioned another incident that took place on the same day George Floyd lost his life: the 911 call made by Amy Cooper against a bird-watcher in New York's Central Park. The world bore witness to the life drained out of a man for what was reported to be eight minutes and forty-six seconds by the police officer who kneeled comfortably on top of his neck, and to hysterical and fallacious claims made by a white female insurance portfolio manager to police about her life being threatened by a Black man named Christian Cooper (no familial relation despite the chilling irony of a shared surname)—when in reality, Christian Cooper's life was the one that hung in the balance as Amy Cooper consciously leveraged a violent police state to do her bidding.

The Cooper case in particular captured white attention in a corporate context because of the relatability of Amy Cooper as an unsuspecting, self-proclaimed liberal and financial professional. Given the damning recorded evidence in both events, neither story could be manipulated, as is often the case, to suggest the culpability of the Black life in jeopardy and justify the execution of violence. Exceptional to these cases, there was no footnote of implied Black criminality; many understood these events simply as wrong.

These events in 2020, coupled with a shift in corporations to prioritize *both* shareholder value and the interests of stakeholders, produced a new level of pressure and scrutiny that inspired corporate America's moral reckoning. And the race on Wall Street to be the first sector, or at least among the first, to set the tone for adjudicating these wrongs further intensified this moment in the corporate world and Black professional participation within it.

Black buy-in or opt-out and the messy in-betweens are emblematic of a larger phenomenon of Black participation in capitalism that structures daily life and informs all forms of activism, or the lack thereof, in the workplace. In Allan's words, "Black responsibility is doing what you can in an imperfect situation. We all should contribute however we can to create better outcomes"—in both our personal and professional lives.

The enduring question of the freighted role as change agent for the Black professional is omnipresent. This begins with my free coaching of a CEO of a multibillion-dollar asset advisory firm. It continues with the expectation of a white senior leader that internal corporate transformation rests on the shoulders of the (nonexistent) Black professionals in her organization. But it exists most loudly, most exhaustedly, in our own internalized ideas about what we as Black professionals owe ourselves and our communities—and by extension our workplaces—in terms of the breadth and depth of our labor. While there is no single answer or way forward that will accommodate the demands of varied corporate cultures, what is certain is that true and total change cannot depend exclusively on Black professional buy-in. We must all buy in to create new structures of being.

Relying on Black professionals to rectify the structures of oppression invariably reiterates the exploitation of their labor, the lack of compensation for their extracurricular professional work, and the uncertainty that their work will even be seriously taken up in a corporate response.

In the words of Laura Morgan Roberts and Ella F. Washington in a 2022 *Harvard Business Review* article, which was shared by Allan on his LinkedIn page, "Racism isn't just Black people's problem; it's everyone's problem because it erodes the fabric of society. Leaders at every level must use their power, platforms, and resources to help employees and communities overcome these challenges and build a better world for us all."[17] These challenges, which have enduring histories on Wall Street, have produced structural forms of inequity that, quite frankly, demand everyone's buy-in to manifest true transformation both in and out of the workplace.

But there are material factors that make it risky for Black professionals to take on partial responsibility for creating a more equitable world. In addition to the potential problems linked to Black professional buy-in (e.g., a lack of compensation, labor exploitation, and a lack of genuine corporate interest) is the reminder of past financial conditions that can motivate one to be silent during critical moments.

For those who enter Wall Street exclusively for its shelter from economic precarity, occupying space in its undercommons looks like producing exceptional work, keeping one's head down, and mouth shut. Strategic acts of assimilation allow one to hold on to newfound economic security and financial freedom. Dennis, whose childhood was marked by poverty, makes the daily choice to prioritize the freedom of financial stability rather than engage in high-risk efforts to inspire corporate cultural change.

The Fear of Poverty

When Dennis and I first sat down to talk about his life on Wall Street over hot plates of Nigerian jollof rice, he told me a short story that simply captures his most important desire in life:

> My manager pulled me into his office for my annual review meeting and said to me: "You're a top performer and I'm pleased with the work you've done thus far. Aside from your bonus, which matches your performance, is there anything else we can do to keep you happy?" I asked him to promote me to associate, to which he laughed and said, "I can't do that quite yet. . . . Do I have to worry about losing you?" I shook my head and quickly said no, to which he said, "Why is that?" both in amusement and as a way for him to indirectly ask what I like about the firm. Through laughter I responded: "Because I don't want to be poor."

Born in Nigeria and raised humbly, Dennis respected the fact that his parents chose lifelong careers in academia—his mother a botanist and his father a zoologist. But despite how honorable his parents' scholarly pursuits were, the thin floor mats they slept on and the limited money for food and school fees was proof they had nothing to show for it. This produced in Dennis a longing for economic advancement that he and his family could enjoy. Neither greed nor power was the rationale for his employment at Goldman Sachs; rather, it was poverty.

When Dennis was offered an internship from the firm to make a six-figure salary as a coder at the age of twenty-one, even though he had never coded before, he said yes. Dennis regularly admits to "drinking the Kool-Aid," acting as the poster child for Goldman Sachs culture, and taking advantage of career opportunities despite feeling exploited at times by how the firm puts his racial diversity on display.

Judging Dennis's choice to accumulate wealth on Wall Street of all places is tempting, especially when paired with the common belief that participating in capitalism produces more harm than good. But whether Dennis's decision is good, bad, or something in between is irrelevant. What matters is recognizing the drivers that produced the decision and, in effect, Dennis's practice of Black Capitalism. As a Black man in America, Dennis feels most financially secure in a predominantly white workplace. Dwelling in the undercommons comes with its own set of ethical concessions. But despite this, Black professionals derive productive meaning from their position at the epicenter of capital production. Black Capitalist thriving on Wall Street is the everyday practice of Black people occupying unlikely spaces to advance themselves and their communities.

The desires and challenges of Black Capitalists who occupy Wall Street's undercommons come alive in Alex, Chris, Allan, and Dennis. Their experiences track the individual and communal process of creating purpose out of one's employment in the finance industry. Meanwhile, another meaningful encounter I

had with a member of the undercommons inspired my exploration of the *afterlives* of Black Wall Streeters.

Now a retired millionaire in his mid-forties, Kwaku spent his
entire professional career at JPMorganChase's Investment Banking Division. But as a Ghanaian American born in Ghana with
deep ties to the country, he's committed himself to serving his
homeland. Kwaku's story is emblematic of a growing phenomenon of Black Capitalists who are looking to Africa, namely
Ghana, with dreams to transform its financial landscape with
the tools and skills they acquired on Wall Street.

As Kwaku's story reveals, a Black identity is not just a racial
distinction but also a social position that ties to someone's ethnic background. For Africans who immigrate to the United
States, the feeling of being relegated to the lowest rung of the
social hierarchy because of their Black identity is experienced in
two ways: first, as a Black person in America forced to confront
the legacy of structural racism that has produced the racial
wealth gap among other phenomena that disproportionately affect Black people, and second, as a Black African in a world
where powerful Western perceptions of Africa produce harmful
beliefs and behaviors about the continent, its people, and its international influence. The social position into which such people are cast shapes their dreams and motivations that affect how
they participate in capitalism.

Africa's Currency in Its Diaspora

"I learned from an early age from my parents that the ticket to
achieve success was education," Kwaku recalled during our first
chat. That fact would alter the trajectory of his professional

career. He was born in Kumasi, Ghana, where he lived with his grandparents until the age of eight. He then moved to New Jersey, where he still lives today. Growing up during the crack epidemic that ravaged many of the Black American communities he called home, he feels lucky to have avoided the temptation and credits his parents' strictness, passion for education, and sacrifice for the life he enjoys today. Kwaku's father worked for Dean Witter and his mother was an administrative clerk. Despite finite resources, his parents enrolled him at the local private Catholic school.

With the support of A Better Chance, a nonprofit organization that helps talented students of color gain admittance and thrive in the nation's premier college preparatory schools, Kwaku attended Rodner High School. It was an experience that woke him up to the reality of his socioeconomic position. "Growing up, all of our parents worked and looked after each other's kids whenever needed. No one was rich, but we were all okay and because everyone was in the same boat, you didn't think about it so much. Going to Rodner was a stark economic change and exposed me to what it meant to be 'rich-rich' and the fact that I wasn't," he recalled through laughter. His matriculation into Brown University four years later further heightened his awareness of economic disparities. But rather than be discouraged by his position, he leaned into what he describes as "the exciting possibilities that the world opened up in college." Guided by his childhood interest in business, Kwaku studied economics, which grew his curiosity in Wall Street and the different kinds of financial services. He took a liking to the world of investment banking.

Kwaku started his first job on Wall Street in the summer of 1997 as an analyst in JPMorganChase's Equity Capital Markets group, led by Jes Staley, the former CEO of Barclays. Supporting the execution of firm-managed initial public offerings (IPOs) required long workdays. Despite the intensity of his early days, Kwaku recounted his experience with a deep sense of nostalgia. He described his first six months as a very scary time in which he couldn't afford to make a mistake. As a result, he worked long days and nights, going home only to shower, change, and get a quick nap. The culture was cutthroat, and no one could rest on their laurels. "In that way, I felt like it was a meritocracy at its core. Wall Street is very quantitative. At the end of the day, what matters is the business you bring to the firm," he recalled.

But there were obstacles to bringing in more business to the firm. At one point, Kwaku managed the firm's oil and gas business, and it took him months to be successful because he had to work at building a rapport with older white men with whom he had little in common. His strategy for success came through observing that visibility was important. The movers and shakers were the ones who were perceived as people who could deliver. Being vocal and confident was essential. "I learned that when I walked into a room to present, the question on people's minds was, 'Is he in command of the room?' Building trust and confidence in clients meant proving my competence through the things I said and how I said it."

This put into perspective for Kwaku how Ghanaian culture—where children are taught to be "softer and more subservient"—can be the biggest obstacle to success for others. Luckily, his exposure and mentorship from Jes helped him break the mold. "I wasn't shy," he recalled. "I was super proactive, always asking questions, which made me coachable and gave people a reason to invest in me." Kwaku learned that on Wall Street, you must be "hard charging." He treated work as a game that he aimed to win. Performance acting was the biggest part of the game. In fact, the "acting" advice came from his white colleagues. He learned to approach work as 90 percent drama and a performance that required persuasion and a mastery of his craft.

The strategies Kwaku adopted for more than two decades afforded him the comfortable, upper-middle-class lifestyle he enjoys with his wife and two kids. He trained himself in the tactics needed to thrive on Wall Street while keeping his homeland close to heart. Kwaku's passion about the economic development of Ghana inspired his current pro bono endeavors, and his desire to serve stems from a long family history of civic engagement in the country. Kwaku's grandfather served as the Bank of Ghana's first director, which was responsible for financing Ghana's independence from Britain. And his father was once a senior ranking official in the military. Today, Kwaku serves on the board of organizations revolutionizing Ghana's healthcare system and on the Ministry of Finance's investment advisory committee.

He uses his advisory role as a platform to enact his hopes for Ghana: to shift from a lower-middle-income to an upper-middle-income country, mitigate poverty, create meaningful jobs for youth, and establish a thriving economy that positions Ghana as the premier hub for commerce in sub-Saharan Africa. Should leaders be able to implement a disciplined strategy to manage the economy, he sees promise in Ghana's stable rule of law, steady infrastructure development, and growing global business mentality. He takes pride in his work with some of the world's most influential Black Capitalists to transform Ghana's and, by extension, the continent's economic landscape. This endeavor was made possible through his occupation in the undercommons of Wall Street.

CHAPTER 3

The Language of Black Capitalism

"Hello?" I said tentatively, assuming Abdul's call was an accidental dial since we had chatted at length just the day before. Abdul was executive director in Morgan Stanley's Investment Banking Division. He and I had met through our mutual social circles and become fast friends, often discussing the intersection of his Wall Street experience, Sierra Leonean heritage, and Black Capitalist identity.

He responded to my greeting with a question: "Do you want to go to the Hamptons tomorrow?"

I laughed at the absurdity of the question and waited a few seconds for him to explain. He didn't.

"Just for fun?" I prodded.

"Yeah, why not? For pure enjoyment's sake. I mean, my birthday is in a few days if you need an excuse to enjoy life, though," he added through a fit of laughter.

Embarrassed by my need to justify an impromptu weekend

in the Hamptons as I listened to Abdul explain logistics, I quickly interjected: "I'm down, let's go."

I spent the rest of that Thursday evening scrambling to get the work done I had planned to do over the weekend, which included writing a section of my dissertation, prepping my business's e-commerce orders for the upcoming week, and finalizing plans for my pop-up Plantain Party at Soho House. The embarrassment I felt while talking to Abdul not only inspired me to rearrange my schedule but also got me thinking. Why did I need a reason to simply have some fun, if I could afford to do so?

While the hustler in me whispered, "Have you earned it? Have you overworked yourself enough this week that a last-minute break is deserved?" Thankfully, my voice of reason interceded, reminding me of the extensive therapy sessions I've had about prioritizing rest, seeking out fun, and understanding what having joy means to me. But the hustler had the last word: "You'll make it up next week," it said. Despite the image of my disappointed therapist in my head, I cosigned the mandate. I would go to the Hamptons physically but be in my work mentally, planning aggressive to-do lists, and go hard the following week. At least I'd be there in person, right?

The next afternoon, Abdul's friend Cliff and two passengers picked me up from my Bed-Stuy apartment in a sleek black Porsche. Kendra was a Sierra Leonean working in higher education, Maxwell a Congolese city planner, and although Cliff was Jamaican, he claimed Ghana via his Ancestry.com results.

Sitting in traffic for most of the two-hour trip, we shared work-related horror stories, professional aspirations, investment strategies, and details about the more "lit" parties and venues we'd been to recently. It was no surprise that Cliff, who was decked out—literally from snapback to sneakers—in clothes from *The Marathon* by Nipsey Hussle, had Hussle's *Victory Lap* album blasting in the background. Kendra and I bopped our heads from the backseat while Cliff and Maxwell rapped along to the lyrics from the song "Grinding All My Life": "Don't know a nigga like myself. I say self-made meaning I designed myself. . . . Damn right I like the life I built. I'm from Westside 60 shit I might got kilt."[1]

This soundtrack set to the moment we were living—young, ambitious Black professionals cruising in a Porsche to a weekend in the Hamptons debating stock picks, Peleton memberships, and the pros and cons of employment at one Fortune 500 company versus another—was both ironic and accurate.

Ironic in that none of us as the children of strict immigrant parents intimately knew the street life Hussle rapped about even though we nodded and sang along as if we did. And yet accurate in its message glorifying the hustle, sacrifice, success, and self-fashioning that comes with a life of grinding to succeed. The music was a reminder that systemic racism against Black people keeps the possibility of falling into poverty precariously close at all times. The aesthetics of our Hamptons trip was evidence of that, too.

When we arrived, the driveway to the mansion where we'd stay was full of luxury cars, each owned by a young Black professional. All weekend, we wined and dined without concern for expense. We talked about power moves—both personal and professional, as well as investing in domestic and international multiuse real estate, securing six-figure consulting contracts, and capitalizing on the tax benefits associated with owning limited liability companies. I was surrounded by high-performing, type-A workaholics who looked like me. But instead of feeling at home, the conversations I had left me anxiously wondering, "Am I doing enough?"

"Doing enough" in order to do, or achieve, what exactly? Well, if I'm honest, to secure and sustain a lifestyle of ease and comfort as quickly as possible. For me, this urgent need for economic security derived from the lingering possibility of being abruptly swept back into a cycle of financial instability. This remains a common reality for many Black people in America because of structural racism and its impact on socioeconomic mobility. So to be blunt, the lifestyle I sought after required money. *Lots* of it.

The pressures and practices of capitalism infected our mindsets and desires that weekend. But surprisingly, the words *capitalism* and *capitalist* were never mentioned over the course of our Hamptons trip. Instead, the words *hustle* and *grind* were used to rationalize the materialism, the acquisition of wealth, and the power and privilege surrounding us. But the hustle culture and the grind mentality are merely permutations and outcomes of one's active participation in capitalism, though they are also specific to Blackness in America.

The Enslaved Capitalist and the Birth of Black Banking

Hustle and *grind* are words that best describe how Black people have taken proactive action within the American political economy dating back to the antebellum period, and the behaviors associated with these popularized terms are nothing new. The relationship between race and capitalism, and what was required of Black people to create opportunities for themselves and thrive within the political economy, has always been complex.

Juliet E. K. Walker's articles "Racism, Slavery, and Free Enterprise" and "Black Entrepreneurship" provide original insight into the lived experience of enslaved people who doubled as "creative capitalists."[2] Walker challenges convention by explaining how "paradoxically, the need to protect private property, which protected and promoted the institution of slavery, also provided the basis for black entrepreneurial expression, both slave and free. The profit motive, underscoring the expansion of America's antebellum economy, also encouraged the expression of black entrepreneurial talent."[3]

Walker quotes the economist Joseph Schumpeter, who emphasized that the "creative capitalist" is driven by both monetary success and "the will to conquer, the impulse to fight, to prove oneself superior to others, to succeed for the sake, not of the fruits of success but of success itself."[4] Despite the racial hierarchy of the time, the white business community created marginal space for antebellum Black entrepreneurship to flourish because, quite frankly, it was profitable.[5] It was more lucrative than not for slave masters to allow enslaved men and women with notable talents and industriousness to buy back their time in pursuit of entrepreneurial endeavors.[6] The business activity of enslaved Black entrepreneurs was yet another way for their slave masters to increase their wealth and generate an even higher return on investment for their property.

Examples of antebellum Black entrepreneurship vary. During the War of 1812, an enslaved man named Free Frank contracted his time to build a saltpeter factory in Kentucky that was tremendously profitable, because saltpeter was a key ingredient in the creation of gunpowder.[7] And with manufacturing limitations in the region, demand was high for Free Frank's product.[8] Free Frank was able to purchase the freedom of his wife in 1817, and his own freedom two years later at the age of forty-two for a sum of $1,600.[9] He went on to expand his saltpeter enterprise, speculate in land, establish a farm, and found a town called New Philadelphia in Illinois.[10] Before his death in 1854, Free Frank purchased freedom for sixteen of his enslaved family members, paying more than $14,000 out of the income generated from his ventures.[11]

Simon Gray was a successful riverboat captain who skillfully managed the end-to-end operations of lumber delivery to plantations in New Orleans and neighboring markets.[12] At the property of Brown Lumber Company, Gray earned a salary of $20 per month and was given full authority to employ members of his crew, made up of ten to twenty men who were Black and white, enslaved and free.[13] In 1855, Gray was granted permission by the company to launch a riverboat business of his own, at which he employed another enslaved man who was a self-hired bondsman.[14] It was often the case that successful Black employers like Gray, enslaved or free, would hire enslaved people to support their businesses, which created opportunities for economic advancement and the pursuit of freedom, otherwise unavailable.[15]

Born into slavery in Virginia in 1818, Elizabeth Keckley was known for her rare talent as a seamstress and fashion designer. She would remain enslaved for more than thirty years until she was able to buy her freedom for $1,200 from the proceeds of her dressmaking business.[16] After moving to Washington, D.C., Keckley became known for being the dressmaker for President Abraham Lincoln's wife, First Lady Mary Todd, and employing twenty seamstresses to meet customer demand.[17] Additionally, her care for the condition of formerly enslaved people would inspire her philanthropic efforts, which gained the support of prominent leaders, including Frederick Douglass, Wendell Phillips, and the first family of the United States.

The respect and recognition of others—Black or white, enslaved or free—was one outcome for Black entrepreneurs who achieved exceptional business success during the antebellum period. For this reason, many Black leaders were staunch supporters of entrepreneurship to "lift" the race out of poverty and, in turn, improve the social, political, and economic standing of the Black community.[18] Access to monetary capital meant access to a kind of power that could not be ignored. And it would take power for Black people to subvert the structural norms that produced the racial landscape of the period.

The tension of Black Capitalism during this time, particularly for the enslaved, was how to successfully pursue entrepreneurship while remaining someone else's property. Enslaved entrepreneurs doubled as bondsmen who hired their own time and depended on human capital resources to support their nascent businesses.[19] "Their investment costs," Walker writes, "were ingenuity, energy, industriousness, resourcefulness, and a formidable business acumen, particularly for those who established the more successful business enterprises."[20] Wages earned went toward startup capital. And, Walker continues, "the profits earned by slave entrepreneurs in their business, after they paid their owners for allowing them to hire their own time, were used primarily as venture capital to purchase freedom for themselves, their family members, or friends."[21] The history of these Black entrepreneurs who subversively used the tools of capitalism to manifest freedom defies historical images that exist in our social imagination about Black life during the era of slavery.

To outperform their white competitors in the market, Black entrepreneurs—enslaved or free—needed exceptional strategic risk-taking skills, experience, and a knack for innovative think-ing. The most successful Black business owners were the ones who created something new—products, production techniques, and markets—or streamlined the distribution of goods.[22] Some of these creative capitalists would generate personal wealth worth more than $100,000 in the period between 1830 and 1860.[23] The existence of Black entrepreneurs in America before the Civil War proves just how long and intensely Black people have been grinding in this country to wake up on the right side of capitalism.

◆ ◆ ◆

Black banking from the antebellum to the postbellum period is another example of how Black people have operated as capital-ists with a nuanced approach out of necessity. Mehrsa Barada-ran's book *The Color of Money* describes the "separate and unequal" banking system for Black and white Americans.[24] She argues that "the hand that drives black poverty is not a natural and invisible one, but rather the coercive hand of the state that has consistently excluded blacks from full participation in American capitalism."[25] Against all odds, Black Americans strove to participate in the American capitalist system as they made the transition from being capital to becoming capitalists in the mid-nineteenth century.[26] The economic landscape of the time was as such:

> Between 1820 and the Civil War, banks across the South issued notes with images of slaves printed on the money. The currency of the South was the slave. Slaves were not just the labor in the cotton production process; they were

the collateral used to finance the operations. Slavery modernized credit markets, creating complex new forms of financial instruments and trade networks through which slaves could be mortgaged, exchanged, and used as leverage to purchase more slaves. In highly profitable, speculation-based markets, many white men built fortunes trading in slave-backed securities. As is true of property ownership in any era, those who held slaves had the ability to grow exponentially richer because they could use their property to create more wealth.[27]

After emancipation in 1863, legitimate banking options for Black people were rare. The Freedmen's Savings Bank, chartered by the U.S. government, became a beacon of hope for the Black community working to achieve upward mobility. But all confidence placed in the bank was abandoned when its true aims were made clear—to be, Baradaran writes, "a savings bank, a teaching institution, rooted in a paternalistic and condescending mission of instructing Blacks in the ways of thrift and capitalism. But the bank left out the most important part of capitalism—the part where capital is able to grow and multiply through credit. By not lending to depositors, the Freedmen's Bank was counterfeit capitalism from its inception."[28]

A government-backed hoax of epic proportions, the Freedmen's Bank and its collapse—which left many customers penniless—catalyzed an interest in Black business participation within the Black community. The bank had been poorly managed for years by scheming white men such as Henry Cooke, who secretly used the hard-earned savings of Black people to finance highly risky, speculative investments that raided the bank of millions of dollars of deposits that were not insured.[29]

The very men entrusted to safeguard the deposits of thousands of Black Americans robbed the bank—without penalty. On June 29, 1874, the bank closed its doors "leaving 61,131 depositors without access to nearly $3 million in deposits," Baradaran writes. "More than half of accumulated black wealth disappeared through the mismanagement of the Freedmen's Savings Bank."[30]

Frederick Douglass, Booker T. Washington, W. E. B. Du Bois, and other leaders encouraged the Black community to leverage its own skills to grow Black commerce in response to the government's refusal to economically support America's Black population. Baradaran quotes Du Bois: "Of all disgraceful swindles perpetuated on a struggling people, the Freedmen's Bank was among the worst, and the Negro did well not to wait for justice but went to banking himself as soon as his ignorance and poverty allowed."[31]

According to Arnett G. Lindsay's 1929 article "The Negro in Banking," by the mid-1800s conventions were taking place across the nation to strategize Black economic improvement and Black businessmen were becoming pioneers in the private banking field. Many leaders of this movement were "successful capitalists, brokers, businessmen and clerks before and after the Civil War."[32] They held business expertise in a range of industries from dry goods import and export to retail and capital lending.[33] But the private banking services these Black pioneers created ultimately lacked the access to capital that white banks received for restructuring during times of nationwide financial crisis.[34]

Even so, collective interest in establishing Black commercial banks remained strong. Booker T. Washington galvanized the popular belief that racial equity could only be achieved through Black ownership of skills, businesses, and real estate, and was a dogged believer in the productive possibilities of capitalism for Black Americans. His road map to equality, prosperity, and personal virtue included free-market capitalism, property ownership, and bootstrap entrepreneurship.[35] And he espoused the belief that hard work led to wealth, and wealth could lead to the defeat of Jim Crow. Owning a bank account, property title, or business became a symbol of Black faith that the fight for racial equality could be won.[36]

Washington has been critiqued for his political beliefs that many claim minimize the challenge racism plays in Black people's ability to equitably participate in capitalism. However, his writings, including *My Larger Education* and *The Future of the American Negro,* would prove he wasn't making light of the effects of white supremacy, but rather urging Black people to not give up the fight for economic advancement. It's why he argued that "the best way to get on well with people is to have something that they want. . . . Nothing else so soon brings about right relations between the two races in the South as the commercial progress of the Negro."[37] Washington's beliefs remain important because the language of "bootstrap entrepreneurship" and industrialism that shifted the mindsets of many Americans, Black and white, then and now, reveals that one-way Black Capitalist activity has always been at work. We just haven't been intentional about calling that activity what it is: *capitalism.*

You Can't Have Your Cake and Eat It Too

Within the Black community, many struggle or refuse to identify as a capitalist because of the moral and ethical implications attached to the taboo title. Despite this, many still intentionally practice the behaviors of capitalism. Viral terms like *hustle culture,* the *soft life* (a wellness initiative that rejects the hustle), and Black Girl Luxury aspire to rebrand our capitalistic activities. We've created filtered ways to talk around—and mask—the enduring fear of what it may reveal about us if we call our behaviors what they really are. Why is that?

History informs so much of our understanding of and relationship to our political economy. We carry with us the intergenerational experience of being laborers in America and can name the ways we feel about the drivers of the racial wealth gap at work in our lives. Though devastating, there's solidarity in this and an abstract common enemy to blame. On the other hand, wearing the capitalist label requires us to take some ownership of the economic system we all take part in today. And with that comes the uncomfortable feeling of culpability—we're on the hook for the multiple forms of inequality that capitalism (re)produces, and more important, we must do something about it. If we buy into the generative potential of capitalism in our own lives, given the mass appeal of hustle culture and soft living, we must reckon with its destructive potential too.

Often when Black people *do* proactively and strategically participate in the political economy, they must justify their choice to engage (to Black and white people alike) as if it's inherently or instinctively wrong to do so. Consider what the rapper and entrepreneur Jay-Z said in response to the romanticization of ideals like the American Dream and "pulling yourself up by your bootstraps": "All these lies that America told us our whole life and then when we start getting it, they try to lock us out of it. They start inventing words like 'capitalist.' We've been called 'niggers' and 'monkeys' and 'shit.'"[38] Jay-Z makes the case that being called a capitalist in America is akin to being called a nigger.[39]

Under the guise of hustling, grinding, or even soft living, capitalist practice can look like having a six-figure job, driving the luxury whip, running a business (or several), and traveling at a moment's notice, all without the label of "capitalist" attached. All the benefits, and none of the drawbacks. But practices of Black Capitalism are as diverse as Black people. A Black Capitalist can also look like a single Black mother working two jobs to afford a home in the best school district in town.

To be a Black Capitalist is not to disavow other possible modes of living. It's using the current mode of living we have— capitalism—to create new futures. Because no matter your current socioeconomic status, and regardless of your race, if you ascribe to hustle culture, the grind mentality, or soft living and luxury—or whiteness—you have an expectation about what your engagement with capitalism can provide you. And that expectation centers on a transactional exchange. In return for your time and labor, or someone else's for that matter, you'll receive the capital needed to materially aid and advance your well-being by satisfying your basic need for food, clean water, and shelter. With regard to race and shelter, it's important to note just how significant having access to capital can be to increase one's physical safety, as being both Black and poor remains especially dangerous.

A refusal to define our capitalist behaviors as such is attractive in part because it absolves us from the moral or ethical obligations we have to one another and allows us to focus on our own self-advancement regardless of the cost to communal well-being. But if we name the capitalist logic embedded in our daily economic encounters, and the hopes we have for our financial futures, we can begin to understand and assume the responsibility that comes with a conscious relationship to capitalism that is sustainable, communal, and in service of social good.

◆ ◆ ◆

A deep dive into the culture of hustling helps us understand how, where, and why monetary capital shows up in the culture and to what end. If you look up the word *hustle* in the *Oxford Advanced Learner's Dictionary*, you'll find the definition is "to make somebody move quickly by pushing them in a rough aggressive way," usually with intent to sell or obtain something.[40] However, the meaning and connotation of the word have shifted over time. In the late nineteenth and early twentieth centuries, *hustle* referred to "gumption" or "hard work" but was associated with illegal activities such as sex work, stealing, and scamming.[41] As the twentieth century progressed, hustling became associated with Blackness and how Black Americans in large numbers secured the means to survive in the face of economic hardship and racism.[42] From the 1990s into the early 2000s, Black rappers reappropriated the word and made the practice culturally cool. It became a fixture of Black life, especially for Black men, who claimed that hustle culture is a requirement for success.[43]

Cue Rick Ross. His 2006 record "Hustlin'" and the official music video put Black hustling on full display. At the start of the video, upbeat Latin music plays in the background as bikini-clad women walk around a vibrant and colorful downtown Miami along Ocean Drive. The pristine boardwalk, beautiful skyline, and massive cruise boats set the backdrop. Ross's husky voice overlays the visual and describes the scene as a "playboy's paradise" filled with "pretty girls and fast cars."[44] But we soon learn that Ross's Miami is not the one we're introduced to at the start of the video. The music switches to a harder, dramatic beat, and the lively colors that animated all the people and objects in the video turn to shades of brown as we watch Ross in a white BMW cross over to *his* Miami in Dade County—where the hustle happens.

As he crosses the literal railroad tracks, we enter what looks like a fraught Black community. A Black woman aggressively sells water bottles in the street as cars drive by, while another woman sells produce to passersby from the back of a fully stocked van. As Ross drives around town, we see Black hustling personified: Young boys sell M&M's on street corners, men pull money out of their shoes to make undisclosed business transactions, and the assumed manager at the car wash is seen both shining and swapping cars to customers. We catch sight of a male co-owned mobile perfume shop in the middle of a live demo. One of the men is propped in the sunroof of the car with his product on display around him as he gives the pitch. The other energetic entrepreneur sprays fragrance on the wrist of a curious customer. Their business strategy proves successful as we then see the entrepreneur and customer exchange a perfume box for cash.

With every location change, as Ross makes his way around his Miami, we see evidence of micro markets where business transactions are conducted and cash is exchanged. What is purchased isn't always clear. But the hustle portrayed runs the gamut from car buying, selling, and swapping to merchandise and fashion. At one point, Ross buys a pair of pressed navy jeans off the street that he slings over his shoulder while walking and rapping. Ross's primary role in the video is to patronize his community of hustlers—no hustle is too small for recognition. Everyone, from children to elders, visually embodies the chorus of Ross's track, "Every day I'm hustlin'."

The video argues there's pride in the hustle and the ingenuity required to build a profitable business with limited resources. But more important, the implied need to survive by any means necessary is what drives the entrepreneurial creativity and innovation. When we strip away the cultural coolness and glorification associated with hustle culture today, we see clearly that creating markets to gain access to money, and using that capital to create economic security, is the crux of the hustle.

It's also worth noting that as *hustle* became fully absorbed into the mainstream lexicon and was no longer a pejorative term associated with people of color—like anything popular *and* Black—white America appropriated the term and the idea, renaming it *gig culture* and the *gig economy*. A *gig* is now interchangeable with a *hustle*.

Sizing the growing global gig economy of today contextualizes just how pressing an issue economic security is within capitalism. According to *Forbes*, in 2023 the market size of the gig economy grew by 17 percent to approximately $455 billion.[45] By 2027, gig workers will account for 50 percent of the U.S. workforce alone.[46] And studies estimate that there will be 79.6 million gig workers by 2025 and 90.1 million by 2028.[47] We also know that 88 percent of the global gig economy's gross volume derives from ridesharing and asset-sharing platforms like Uber and Airbnb, respectively.[48] These digital platforms are sustained by three key roles: the provider, consumer, and enabler. The provider produces a service (physical or virtual labor) that the consumer buys, and that transaction is permitted through the digital infrastructure the enabler creates.

Unsurprisingly, the supply of labor is largely concentrated within the Global South (a term that refers broadly to the regions of Africa, Asia, Latin America, and Oceania that are perceived as "underdeveloped," where providers have a greater reliance on gig work to combat enduring structures of economic precarity.[49] If we take Ghana as a case study, the labor force in the country was approximately 11 million people ages twenty-five and older as of 2022.[50] In that same year, close to 7.5 million people remained employed throughout the year, leaving 3.5 million people moving in and out of short-term employment (i.e., the gig economy).[51] Why does this matter? Some quick math proves that 32 percent (and growing!) of Ghana's entire labor force is hustling to make ends meet within capitalism. A day in the life of a gig worker can look like driving Uber by daybreak, washing cars by midday, and selling electronics by night.

But when it comes to the hustle, location matters. The look and feel of hustle culture is different depending on location and indicates the level of privilege people have access to within the space they occupy. Hustling in the streets of Miami-Dade County is a different experience from hustling in the marketplace of Accra or in the corporate offices of New York City. Those who hustle in the street or in the office (or anywhere else for that matter) can share common desires for wealth accumulation, economic security, and greater opportunities in life, but the context through which they hustle matters. For some, hustling is positioned as a choice, albeit with costs, whereas for others, hustling is the sole means for survival.

One of my research trips to Ghana revealed what the hustle to survive can look like in the lives of locals. Heading home to my Airbnb in East Legon after a long day of participant observation at a social enterprise company, I booked an Uber ride from the city's A&C Mall. My driver, Kofi, was already on-site waiting for a ride request in the parking lot, and we quickly found each other and were off for the twenty-minute ride.

The well-kept black Toyota Camry he was driving was more luxurious than the Uber rides I'd grown accustomed to. King Promise, a Ghanaian singer-songwriter, was singing through the speakers; the windows were rolled up; and the air conditioner was on—a practice many Uber drivers in Ghana avoid because it wastefully burns their fuel. I caught Kofi catching a glimpse of me through his rearview mirror. I smiled, and he took that as an invitation for conversation.

I expected some small talk, but he got straight to the point. "Madame, if you need any charger for your phone, I have, so you just let me know please," he said while gesturing toward a plastic container in the passenger seat filled with Android and Apple chargers, HDMI cords, SIM cards, and other gadgets. "I'm alri . . . ," I began but stopped midsentence as he pitched me his collection of "fine" pillows, bedsheets, roll-on deodorant, and handkerchiefs packaged neatly in his trunk, should I be interested. While I didn't buy any Avon deodorant or knock-off Ralph Lauren bedsheets when he dropped me off, for the remainder of my stay I did occasionally purchase the private driving services that he offered on the Uber platform, which was more lucrative for him and more convenient for me. Kofi's hustle in the Ghanaian market is reflective of the kind of imagination it takes to secure capital in the gig economy, especially as Black and African people.

Hustle culture has its grip on corporate America too, and only in recent years have corporations begun to promote messages about work-life balance to their employees. On the flip side, in an era of grind culture grinding us down to the bone, a growing number of professionals emphasize the need to cancel hustle culture to enhance both business productivity and employee satisfaction. However, prioritizing work-life balance is nowhere near normalized. And until it is, the toxicity of hustle culture in the workplace continues to ravage the physical, emotional, and mental well-being of industry professionals.

Sayings like "Hustle harder" and "Don't stop when you're tired. Stop when you're done" are plastered on office walls, furniture, and random paraphernalia to inspire workers to stay at work.[52] And the sobering truth is that the white-ification of hustle culture evidenced through these glorified yet exploitative labor practices make it harder for all of us—regardless of race—to get ahead.[53] As writer Erin Griffith suggests, our system is broken and to reap maximum benefits from it, you must sacrifice yourself totally.[54] That sacrifice creates the perception of ambition and success. "In the new work culture, enduring or even merely liking one's job is not enough. Workers should *love* what they do, and then promote that love on social media, thus fusing their identities to that of their employers," writes Griffith in her *New York Times* article "Why Are Young People Pretending to Love Work?"[55]

To counteract the harm of racialized capitalism, people like Tricia Hersey, founder of Nap Ministry and author of *Rest Is Resistance,* are reclaiming ownership of their mind and body through intentional restfulness. It's a defensive response to an economic system "created on plantations during chattel slavery," Hersey notes, and in the contemporary moment is "driving the entire globe to exhaustion and a deep disconnection with our bodies and minds today."[56] Hersey makes clear that the mission of her organization is about much more than evangelizing the need for people to take naps:

> My rest as a Black woman in America suffering from generational exhaustion and racial trauma always was a political refusal and social justice uprising within my body. I took to rest and naps and slowing down as a way to save my life, resist the systems telling me to do more and most importantly as a remembrance to my Ancestors who had their DreamSpace stolen from them. This is about more than naps. . . . It is about a deep unraveling from white supremacy and capitalism.[57]

Hersey's "rest as resistance" and "rest as reparations" framework is a guide on how to "deprogram, decolonize, and unravel ourselves from the wreckage of capitalism" we are entangled in today.[58] The chronic anxiety, panic attacks, and insomnia I've endured on account of the pressures of capitalism make Hersey's invitation to intentional restfulness hard to ignore. To be Black and mindful about the need to proactively rest and treat our bodies like the "sites of liberation, knowledge, and invention" that they are, is both an interruption to the grind of capitalism and an invitation for us to reimagine how to operate *in* but not *of* capitalism.[59] A new collective orientation to, and engagement with, capitalism changes the version of capitalism we experience.

Black Capitalism, which accounts for restfulness, is distinct from our shared experience of the kind of capitalism Hersey shepherds us away from. If "rest pushes back and disrupts a system that views human bodies as a tool for production and labor," as Hersey claims, then that pushback and disruption of the system can intervene in and refashion the system itself.[60] The blueprint for the more inclusive version of capitalism we can create together recognizes the humanity of people first and combats the racial and economic inequity the capitalism we know today thrives on.

CHAPTER 4

Champagne, Dice, and Everything Nice

My mom's time in the United States has never been easy. Throughout my childhood she worked two jobs, seven days a week, to provide Dash and me with our basic needs. She raised us alone, and I always felt guilty about her being a single parent. I tried my hardest to cause as little trouble as possible, and I honestly felt relieved when I left home for college because I thought now her life was hers again to explore, to have fun, and do the things that would make her happy.

By the time I was in graduate school, it'd been years since I lived at home. As the last child to leave my mother's house, I assumed she was working less and maybe even quit her part-time job. One day, after class, I called her and casually asked her what she was doing, to which she responded, "I'll get ready for work in a few." Turns out she had taken on additional shifts to fill the time she otherwise would have dedicated to her kids.

I asked if she'd considered going on more walks, trying yoga or the local gym, watching a movie, or anything to treat herself.

She laughed and said, "Ei! What has America done to you?" while pounding her plantain and cassava fufu to pair with her groundnut soup.

My mom's two minimum-wage jobs never produced much in material resources for us, but her work ethic, determination, and hustle made the difference in setting my brother and me up for the privileged lives we live today. Unbeknown to her, my mom's capitalist orientation, shaped by our socioeconomic position, kept her acutely aware of the need to obtain capital to access the kinds of abundant life choices and opportunities that could shift the trajectory of generational wealth creation for our family—both in America and Africa. But the result was also that my mother struggled to understand the benefits of rest.

The American Dream's role in the immigrant narrative demands that to achieve the dream with urgency, you must always be in a state of usefulness and productivity. When I think about my mother's question, I think not about what America has done to me, but about what it has done to her. The hard conditioning that comes with trying to make it in America makes it difficult to see a life beyond the hustle. As the elusive dream suggests, picking yourself up by your bootstraps, working day after day, and surviving by any means necessary is what provides you the resources to materialize the dream—not bubble baths, meditation, and intentional self-care days.

I absorbed much of my mother's mentality by the mere fact of living under her roof for the better part of my life. Years have passed since I've done that, but from time to time I feel like a slacker for not waking up at the crack of dawn to sweep and dust my Brooklyn condo, or do a "pre-study" for the day, as I'd much rather, and often do, sleep in. I justify my own work ethic by recognizing that in comparison to my mom's extreme version, I have a softer approach. The unease, however, is in knowing I can adopt these touches because I can afford it, not just because I choose it. My current six-figure JPMorganChase salary and homeownership don't require me to move through life the way my mom had to.

A unifying belief among Black Capitalists is that, despite the structural racism and common barriers, we should use the tools of capitalism as best we can to create new possibilities of thriving for ourselves and our communities and reject a scarcity mindset. For the Black community, largely accustomed to struggle and injustice, luxurious living presents a challenge to old ways of thinking and being. But this lifestyle is also looked down upon by some because, so often in the Black community, we wear our struggle as a badge of honor. And even in elite spaces of privilege like Yale, I witnessed how people become martyrs to the struggle to garner credibility within the Black community.

Norman and I went to undergrad together at Boston College before I transferred to NYU. He is a brilliant Black scholar with the kind of intellect that everyone thought would land him a career as a professor. We both ended up at Yale for graduate school, and he was two years ahead of me in the African American studies program. He lived in Brooklyn too, and so on one rare day when I saw him on campus I accepted his offer of a ride home, which beat taking the MetroNorth. That day, we talked about how I was adjusting to my program, finding community within my cohort, and making progress on crafting my research project. I gave him the broad strokes of my dissertation, and he listened in silence, eyes glued to the road.

He remained silent after I finished, so I tried to fill the space by addressing what I knew he was thinking: "Yes, I acknowledge the fact that the African American Studies Department at Yale and many across the country were made possible through resistance movements. So I get that a story about Black Capitalists is uncomfortable for all the obvious reasons, but I don't think discomfort should be the reason we don't create knowledge about a phenomenon, especially since its intent is social good."

"Yeah, that's gonna be tough," he finally admitted, "but I understand. Don't tell anyone, but I love luxury and a comfortable lifestyle. So I get the tension."

My guard fell as he opened up to me, but I was a bit alarmed that over the course of our two-hour ride back to the city, he told me three more times to not tell anyone about his love for luxury. Norman studied policing and was a highly visible activist and thought leader on campus and within the Black community. I realized he had an image to uphold. To many, Norman, a staunch advocate for Black liberation, should not also be a lover of the finer things in life—like his membership at an exclusive gym club, passive income from homeownership, and handsome consulting contracts with companies like Google. He was practicing the soft life, while trying to hide the fact.

A soft-life posture presents a different set of life choices than many Black people are used to. Marketed as a wellness initiative, the soft-life movement promotes the importance of rest, self-care, and gentleness specifically among Black women who are constantly combating the strong Black woman narrative and often don't have the time or resources to prioritize their own well-being. It's also a framework that draws a correlation between communal wellness and ethical consumption when conscious consumer behaviors are adopted, like patronizing businesses that value and support social and environmental good. Such practices nurture an environment of ease where more people can thrive.

I struggled in my initial attempts at soft living, and still do. My solo travels across the world are an example of this. Now that I make money, I frequently leave the country, often just to eat. I've gone to Vietnam for a warm bowl of pho, Colombia for a cup of coffee, Thailand for authentic pad see ew, Copenhagen for a buttery pastry, the Maldives for handulu bondibai,[1] and Hawaii for malasadas, to name a few. For me, food is never *just* food. It represents history, communal care, and expressions of cultural identity. Traveling to experience the food of other people in their motherland allows the curious anthropologist in me to better understand people across cultural differences and share a meal in celebration of that difference.

Vacation is part of white life I observed as a child and even now as an adult. I grew accustomed to my white friends, classmates, and colleagues talking about their family summer trips to the beach, or the south of France, or even "exotic" destinations around the world located in the Global South. And travel like this, casual and routine, becomes an Instagram story. But I would never think to be on Instagram throwing dollar bills as if frequent jet-setting is nothing to blush at.

To travel for myself and by myself is the conflict. Being a Black Capitalist means that I get to have these experiences, but it also means that when I travel, I see the things that white people don't. Though I'm vacationing, I still recognize and feel the discomfort of racial difference. I can enjoy that bowl of pho and watch people shamelessly take photos of me because they've never seen a Black person before. Or be on the Ba Na cable car thousands of feet above the ground in Da Nang minding my business while a stranger seated next to me pulls one of my locs into the palm of her hand for close examination—*without* asking. Or be in Cartagena on a historic bike tour along the coast and hear my guide tell me "*You* are the attraction" because of my unusual chocolate skin and natural long locs in a city defined by colorism. Or be at an upscale restaurant in Providenciales and observe the contrast between how I speak with waiters and how some white patrons treat them as if they are invisible. I watch as people perceive my ability to be in these spaces as strange, and I smile back in response, which usually deepens their state of confusion as I revel in these moments of soft living. Such moments can force people to rethink their assumptions about what Black life can look like.

My mom, too, is beginning to discover her right to see the world as her children get richer. "You guys are okay now" is the reason she gives for her surprising change in mindset. And the guarantee is that if her children are okay, she is too. She tells me about her regular road trips, and I listen amazed because growing up, I watched her drive mostly to work, church, the grocery store, and home. Now she leaves me WhatsApp voice notes with soft-life reminders: "Rach-cho-cho! Life is short. Make sure you enjoy it and have fun, okay? You can't work all the time and not enjoy life. And always remember that I love you." My mom's playfulness, leisure, and sense of adventure reflect her own shifting orientation to capitalism on account of her children's. The safety net she has watched Dash and me hustle to build over time and the work ethic she raised us to value allow her to relax without a sense of worry.

But as my indulgences have gotten pricier, I still catch myself in the vicious web of justifying my purchasing decisions to myself. I'm constantly doing the work of reminding myself, as a Black woman, that rest and enjoyment in this lifetime are not only worth the price, but are lifesaving.

❖ ❖ ❖

According to Brianna Holt in her *Insider* article "How Young Black Women Are Manifesting a Soft Life," the viral trend has its origins in the Nigerian influencer community and was conceived as an "alternative to the harsh demands of hustle culture and the labor demands placed on Black women as providers."[2] It offers the most seductive language of capitalism and is often pitted against hustle culture because of its gentler approach to living. Holt quotes Nicole Jenkins, assistant professor of sociology at Howard University:

> Everybody understands self-care, but Black women generally have had a difficult time because they're often prioritizing other folks' needs over themselves. It's a new rendition of self-care that is really unapologetically prioritizing what it is that we need in rejection of this strong woman narrative that so many of us have been cultured into really adopting.[3]

Comfort, leisure, creating boundaries, intentional breathing, greater self-awareness, and recognizing and refusing stress are just some of the hallmarks of soft, sustainable living that are foreign to many Black people, and especially Black women who are accustomed and forced to carry more than their fair share of familial and communal burdens. While modern capitalism implants a "no days off" mentality into our minds that defines the measure of success in our lives, the soft-life feature of Black Capitalism gently reminds us of the importance of reclaiming a posture of restfulness to richly experience life as it should be lived.

It's about "getting us to the point where we are acknowledging that we don't want the struggle life. We don't want the struggle love, we don't want the struggle job, we don't want any of that," argues Devyn Walker, a professional counselor who specializes in working with Black women dealing with trauma.[4] Brittany, a lifestyle blogger and pioneer of the "soft life Black woman" trend on TikTok, has emphatically posted that the "whole strong Black woman narrative . . . doesn't apply to me. I live a soft life. I am a dainty princess. I will fall out at the drop of a minor inconvenience."[5]

But how does one achieve this "dainty," royal lifestyle Brittany champions? Jadriena Solomon, in her *21 Ninety* article "How to Start Living a Soft Life," offers a six-point process to implement a soft-life mentality.

1. Wake up at a time that allows you to get at least thirty minutes of time to yourself.
2. Prioritize yourself and your needs.
3. Create boundaries in your relationships.
4. Incorporate self-care into your life.
   a. Incorporating your favorite beauty products and practices into your weekly routine or daily routine. Set aside a day to just pamper yourself. Take a bubble bath, wash your hair. . . .
5. Don't chase what isn't meant to be.
6. Know your worth.[6]

Across these six commandments of soft living, an intentional and persistent practice of self-care is the recurring theme. Survival is the goal for the strong Black woman, but for the soft

Black girl, *thriving* is the mission.[7] L'Oreal Thompson Payton, in her *Fortune* article "It's Time to Leave the Strong Black Woman Trope in the Past: Meet the Soft Black Girl," makes the point that the trend, with more than five hundred million views of its associated #softlife hashtag, is more than a viral trend about aesthetics. It's a movement that aims to inspire better mental health practices by providing a rare model of Black woman restfulness and relaxation.[8] It follows a school of thought led by self-care advocates who planted the seeds for the movement that exists today. As Audre Lorde once said, "Caring for myself is not self-indulgence, it is self-preservation and that is an act of political warfare."

But what's the admittance price to this soft life of self-preservation replete with pampering, bubble baths, restfulness, and boundary-making? Money and privilege, for sure. Surely, you can adopt the mindset, but if you don't have the life circumstances, which are largely informed by your level of access to discretionary income, materializing the belief system is a futile endeavor. Even more, the pleasures of ethical consumption, which can be a facet of soft living within capitalism—such as buying humanely produced goods, sourcing healthier small-batch and locally grown foods, and exclusively patronizing businesses that have a social responsibility mandate—demand you be rich.

If Black Capitalism is how we hack the system in search of rest, it's because making healthy and sustainable choices is hard to do when you're poor. Before I had a well-paying job, I wasn't buying my favorite organic cotton candy grapes, beautiful hand-woven clothing manufactured by women who are paid a livable wage, or debating which compost machine I should purchase.

What kept me up at night was the thought of getting sick and needing medical attention that I couldn't afford because neither I nor my mom had health insurance. Heavy applications of shea butter, regular spoonfuls of cod-liver oil, and milk of magnesia were our health insurance.

I used to think there was some healing magic in these remedies because, sure enough, my family and I rarely ever got sick. And while I still swear by Ghanaian shea butter, I know my mom was so cautious of our whereabouts and meticulous in our cleanliness and home upkeep because she knew we couldn't afford to get sick, literally.

The truth is that proactively participating in capitalism can unlock access not only to soft living but also to the basic health and wellness resources needed to sustain ourselves and our community. Being a Black Capitalist doesn't mean that one cannot or should not resist what capitalism enables, like access to healthcare, which should be accessible to all people notwithstanding their economic system or their position within it. A conscious practice of Black Capitalism can leverage the resources created in capitalism to further social good while working to critique and alleviate the harms of capitalism and demand it serve people better.

Soft living, with its conscious form of consumption, is a stark contrast to the passive and less costly (to the consumer)—in the short term—method of consumption in which many participate daily. The goods and services we consume under capitalism so often are produced through inhumane means, such as worker exploitation, wage theft, and child labor. Keeping up with the soft lifestyle can be beneficial to all members of the supply chain, but it requires consumers to buy into the value proposition of individual ethical consumption and living wages—and to have the financial wherewithal to do so. Although mental health awareness and wellness are at the heart of the well-intentioned soft-life movement, capital, wealth, and privilege are the engines that drive its varied levels of accessibility at the individual level. There is much to be gained by adopting the soft life, but it'd be naive to assume that it costs one nothing to afford the (im)material benefits it offers.

What struck me while researching the term is its origin in the Nigerian community. As a Ghanaian aware of the stereotypes that plague my fellow West Africans, I jokingly wondered, "But what Nigerian isn't a proud, self-proclaimed hustler?" Every Nigerian I know has mastered the finesse, is collecting all the checks, and somehow surpassed familial expectations and became a doctor, lawyer, and engineer while running their own successful business and faithfully attending church and Bible study three times a week. And they're not even thirty years old! All right, no, I don't know any Nigerians who fit this description exactly (I'm certain they exist, though, and if you're reading this, I see you), but the point is that adopting the soft life in an African immigrant context adds another layer of complexity.

One can have less money at their disposal and find sustainable means to survive and live simply (though money also buys time). However, living on this side of the soft-life spectrum often requires instances of hustle to address unexpected needs or to replenish depleted savings. In my own experience, I resigned from Goldman Sachs feeling secure in the savings I had amassed as I left for a life in academia. But as my graduate school years wore on, I grew more familiar (and uncomfortable) with the bleak job prospects and salary expectations for people with newly minted doctorates. I saw living examples of the stereotypical struggling academic who is a martyr for their work and overzealous to share their socialist manifesto with any available ear.

While I respected and even admired this life choice, I knew with certainty that I needed something different. I began scrolling through LinkedIn job postings, eager to find corporate roles that both aligned with my interests and, yes, paid handsomely. Because honestly, who wants to be broke? When you don't come from money, "getting out" can be a fleeting experience if your engagement with capitalism does not sustain a lifestyle of "staying out." And structural racism makes "staying out" not guaranteed.

◆ ◆ ◆

Despite the structural challenges that remain, soft living now has a viral gendered spin-off called Black Girl Luxury. This movement takes soft living to the next level by insisting that Black women prioritize themselves in lavish ways—a concept foreign to many. Elizabeth Ayoola's *Essence* article, "Embracing Luxury as a Black Woman Has Been Hard—Here Is How I'm Shifting My Mindset," traces the internal work she had to do in order to, first, understand why she criticized women who adopted the lifestyle and, second, learn the value of the lifestyle and ways to embody it on her own terms.

The starting point of Ayoola's perspective on luxury and comfortable living reveals a sobering truth about the relationship Black people can have to capitalism. Just as decades of institutional racism, economic inequality, and labor exploitation are why a brilliant Black Yale doctoral candidate critiqued my work by saying "Black Capitalists don't exist!," American capitalism and its living history make it difficult to imagine a world where Black people can be the beneficiaries of a system they were violently forced to create and sustain. But challenging capitalism's resistance to us expands our capacity to thrive within the system, as well as create forms of Black Capitalism that resist the horrors of the capitalism we know and live in today.

Growing up in a modest and religious home, Ayoola had her needs met, but there was never an air of indulgence because her family, like many other Black families, believed that the love of money was the source of all evil. As she puts it: "I would also make self-righteous comments about people who chose to dress their kids in designer clothes or buy items that cost thousands of dollars. I would remark that they 'should be investing and saving for retirement.'"[9]

Ayoola realized that these projections reflected her scarcity mindset, which revealed her relationship to capitalism. When I read Ayoola's story, I was intrigued by her paradigm shift. Bearing witness to luxurious living can be triggering if unfamiliar, and a scarcity mindset has a lot to do with it. Common questions, like "Do *I* deserve to have my wants and needs met in abundance?" or "Is it right for *me* to thrive?" assume that something about one's makeup excludes one from comfort. In Ayoola's case, that something is race. Black American history shows us more instances of struggle than thriving, and so to believe that thriving is one's birthright calls into question all the evidence we've seen, heard, and learned to the contrary.

When you consider adopting a luxurious lifestyle through the lens of Blackness in America, critiques like that of Tamara Morrison's in her article "The Paradox of the Black Women in Luxury Movement" comes to the fore:

After all, how luxurious is the expensive trip when you're harassed in the airport for wearing a bonnet or having your hair searched on the way there? How luxurious is the handbag you purchased when you were followed around the store the entire time you were shopping for it? How luxurious was the spa when you had to ride to a place where you were the only Black person near for miles? Comfort and elegance is a lot more complex when we enter "luxurious" spaces and the luxury rarely extends to all aspects of our lives.[10]

It's well noted the ways in which Black people are cast as permanent outsiders, even when we have money. Morrison addresses the structural forces at play that can complicate one's enjoyment of a luxurious lifestyle, but society's acceptance, or not, of Black people thriving should not dictate our worthiness of it.

Marshaling the language of luxurious living, much like soft living, absolves us from confronting the justified moral issues, but naming the driver of these trends—an adept and strategic engagement with capitalism to serve one's ends—allows us to hold in tension the responsibility that comes with actively participating in, and benefiting from, an unjust economic system.

Where I come from and the sacrifices my mom made so that I could enjoy some of the simple pleasures of soft living are never forgotten. It's this constant reminder that makes adopting the soft life, while rejecting hustle culture, difficult. Can you obtain a soft life without hustling to get it? Being the child of an African immigrant keeps me rooted in the *cost* of the American Dream and conscious of the fact that this dream is a version of soft living that demands having excess resources to materialize it.

To return to that extravagant Hamptons trip I took with Abdul and other first-generation African Americans, Black

Capitalism is a process that, through its existence, simultaneously retools the version of capitalism we live in today. While we were in a mansion barbequing jerk chicken, leisurely playing Frisbee in the backyard, and dancing to Nigerian rapper Wiz-Kid, I wondered, "How many houses in the Hamptons right now are occupied by rich Black people?" Our rental house was filled with Black people in a starkly white space, and our collective wealth in that moment made us more visible.

The morning after the first night, a few of us made a bagel run to the neighborhood deli and the awkwardness between our group and the white locals and visitors was palpable. My double consciousness split my thinking in half. One stream of thought was: "Mm, vegan cream cheese and jalapeño spread looks good! But maybe I should try the oatmeal special? What was that pool game Abdul said he wanted to play when we get back to the house?" While the other stream of thought was: "I wonder why that middle-aged white couple is staring at me so intently. Surely they've seen a Black woman before? Perhaps not in the Hamptons?" Their gaze felt both curious and uneasy.

This twoness of thought imposed on Black people is separate and distinct. We can enjoy the moments that Black Capitalism allows, like lavish weekend trips with friends without concern for expense, but we are always cognizant of the white gaze. Even though we had the money to be there and afford whatever we wanted, the stares, harmless or otherwise, were a reminder that we are treated as if we don't belong.

Money can't buy your way into psychological or physical safety, which paradoxically reinforces the need to have money to have a fighting chance at security at all. The persistence of the white gaze at the mere presence of Black Capitalists alone troubles preconceived notions about how Black people can relate to our political economy, the spaces they can occupy, and what they can do to change the outcomes of capitalism and who it affects. When it comes to Black Capitalism, and its constant re-engineering of capitalism as we know it, if we look closely, there is something for all of us to learn.

CHAPTER 5

Kelewele

One year into my graduate program at Yale I did something a little bit crazy and decided to start a business. I was reading more than I knew humanly possible, writing countless papers, and commuting from Brooklyn to New Haven weekly because I couldn't bring myself to give up my $1,100 one-bedroom apartment (that's a hustle story for another book). Despite all this, I reasoned that this was the best time to launch my startup Kelewele since my access to Yale's resources for student entrepreneurs—incubators, grants, office hours with industry experts, and summer fellowships—would expire when I graduated. Seizing the moment, and the capital that came with it, is what made me an entrepreneur.

I built Kelewele to be a Ghanaian food service focused on reimagining plantains (think plantain ice cream, cookies, brownies) in its mission to provide familiar yet innovative, vegan, and sustainable products to communities of color. But long before Kelewele was the name of my business, it was and is the name of a popular Ghanaian street food made of spiced and fried sweet plantains served with groundnuts. It was the first plantain dish I had growing up as a child, and I fell in love with the superfood prevalent across the African diaspora and Southeast Asia.

Over time, I had grown to understand food as cultural (re)production. I thought plantains were unique because they symbolized African diasporic foodways. The presence of trans-atlantic cultural ties was evident to me through the similar ways plantains are prepared both on and off the African continent. Through this process the recipe for Kelewele became clear to me: culture, food, migration, and community. While my love for plantains started in the United States (at least, as far as I can re-member), it harks back to the cultural practices of a people an ocean away in Ghana. I was eager to build a food business that was uniquely centered on a single ingredient that was culturally significant and familiar to many, yet innovative, experiential, and most important, brought people together from across the world.

As a graduate student and entrepreneur at Yale, I learned a key lesson: Capitalize on available institutional resources be-cause it's not guaranteed that they'll last forever. I didn't move with the caution that defined my career at Goldman Sachs. In-stead, I operated with a sense of urgency because my six years of full funding at Yale had an expiration date. Presented with the rare opportunity to live cost free, I made it my mission to leave no stone unturned. My practice of capitalism was equal parts strategy, finesse, hustle, and muscle memory.

Leading up to my launch, I hosted Kelewele Kickbacks, which were small gatherings in my apartment where friends could sample my plantain creations. My events were prospective cus-tomer focus groups in disguise—a way to gather feedback on my minimum viable products from people who doubled as my target audience. They grew my understanding of what consumers wanted and my confidence to deliver on that as I refined my products. From there, I scaled up by leveraging a grassroots approach at Brooklyn's four-day International African Arts Festival in Commodore Barry Park, which featured hundreds of Black-owned businesses celebrating African culture. And in the summer of 2018, I'd join them as a vendor.

Serving thousands of people over ninety-six hours with a few friends who volunteered their time to help run my ten-by-ten tent station in ninety-five-degree heat was intense. But the experience produced invaluable research on why plantain lovers would buy my products versus not, how they wanted to consume plantains, where they wanted to buy them, and how they wanted unique products like mine to be marketed to them. I'd go on to vend at festivals like Curlfest, Vegandale, and AfroFuture; take corporate catering gigs; and host local pop-ups of my own in partnership with prominent businesses in the community. I treated these events as low-cost product validation checks that minimized the risk attached to building a business from scratch with limited funds.

I figured my chances of failing were decreased if I knew my customers intimately and I spent the money I had on solving customer needs associated with my products. Staying judicious about spending and close to my customers prompted my next scale-up: e-commerce and wholesale. My customers needed consistent ways to access Kelewele products from anywhere in the country. At this point I was offering hot, cold, and shelf-stable foods, including plantain lasagna, an assortment of ice creams, cookies, and gluten-free brownie mix. E-commerce with nationwide shipping of the shelf-stable products solved the problem, especially for those out of state, and my wholesale partnerships with community cornerstones like Aunts et Uncles, Brooklyn Tea, and GinJan addressed the desire NYC locals had for physical engagement with the brand (even if it was via proxy through my partners).

As Kelewele grew, and with a bit of luck produced by constraints on landlords during COVID, I opened a fast-casual food stall at Dekalb Market Hall—Brooklyn's largest indoor food court—to accommodate demand and stepped into the role of employer for the first time. Soon thereafter Barclays Center tapped me to open a concession stand at the stadium. Kelewele would make history as the first Black woman–owned and fully vegan offering at both Dekalb Market Hall and Barclays Center. To date, assuming the role of employer is the hardest and most exhausting thing I've ever done. I was constantly wondering and worrying about how my actions as an employer would make my employees feel about their own financial future and present. Would working at Kelewele feel like a dead-end job that would give them just enough to scrape by? Would they feel that I was equally invested in their thriving? Or would they feel like they were in a rut on the wrong side of capitalism while I was on the other side? I wanted to do right by the people I employed *and* make money. But the prevailing question was: What does "doing right" mean?

Twenty-seven years old, and with no formal training in restaurant logistics, I pulled together a team that, at its peak, totaled twenty-five people who helped me build financial models, establish a strategy for pricing products, and create an operational model to service customers nine hours a day, seven days a week. That team was in large part funded by Yale, and my finance guru who ran Kelewele's profitability models was a Yale MBA student and incoming investment banking analyst at Citi-Bank. And Yale footed the bill on the acquisition of my two graphic design interns, and a third intern who refined our product pricing methodology and doubled as a salesperson for our business-to-business wholesale distribution channel.

Through Yale, I even had a marketing expert and graphic designer whose work helped get the attention of *The New York Times, MarketWatch,* and *Bloomberg News.* And as a participant in Yale's Tsai CITY Summer Fellowship program, designed to support select student entrepreneurs, and Goldman Sachs's 10,000 Small Businesses incubator, I got direct access to advisors in the food industry who were generous in offering guidance and connections—the kind of social capital crucial to creating and sustaining the strategy of any business. Propelled into the world of ownership and responsible for the well-being of my team, I faced a new set of questions about the ethics of capitalism, and perhaps the most important question of all: What kind of capitalist would *I* be?

I had a host of questions to answer: What is the balance between ethical wages, employee satisfaction (professional development opportunities, time off, and overall happiness), and business profitability? What are the everyday actions that establish and sustain company culture, that minimize environmental harms, and don't replicate the biases of the world—and what was I doing about it? What would it take to create an environment that ruptured conventional understandings of the primary roles within capitalism (the capitalist and the laborer), and allowed for collective economic flourishing? I worried about the possibility of my employees viewing their employment at

Kelewele as a dead end to personal and professional growth. And that they'd clock in every day not because they enjoyed the work or saw nonmonetary value in it, but because there was no better option. I learned just how hard answering these questions can be, and that they require constant iteration and staying honest about the fears, traumas, and desires we all carry about money and our relationship to wealth.

There were instances of happiness in the beginning, but stress, anxiety, and worry largely informed the experience. It never mattered so much *what* I was doing, but rather *why* I was doing it. I want(ed) a better life for myself and my family. A life where, for every decision, I have multiple options and never have to make choices out of desperation. I'm proud of my discipline and determination, but never happy about the fact that I must do the exhausting work of finding cunning ways to simultaneously live my dreams and not worry about having enough. I often joke with friends that I want to take a gap year someday just to rest from all the grinding and the toll it's taken. This is capitalism. In my life, I try to acknowledge the sacrifices I've made to create opportunities for myself, but always leave room to name the privileges inherent in my experience and the responsibility that comes with that—and *this,* I think, is Black Capitalism.

◆ ◆ ◆

During school I had the chance to pitch Kelewele to Barry Nalebuff, the cofounder of Honest Tea. A mentor of mine encouraged me to reach out to Barry, who is also a professor at Yale's School of Management. I didn't know who he was, but I learned that he loved to support students in entrepreneurial pursuits, so I took a shot in the dark and sent him an email asking for fifteen minutes of his time. He responded within five minutes and said, "Funny enough, I've been looking to invest in an ice cream company. Plantain ice cream, that's different. Happy to chat, let me know when you're free."

I read his reply at least ten times before immediately texting my brother, "What should I do?" I had the ear of a successful entrepreneur, and I was determined to make the most of it. After a conversation with Dash, I responded to Barry's email, and we set a date to meet in person the next week. Not only did he put in an order to try *every* single item on my e-commerce website, but he also gave me some pre-reading for us to discuss and requested my pitch deck.

I furiously went to work revamping the deck I had on hand; reading the lengthy book he assigned, which he had written (so I read it cover to cover); and making pints of dairy-free plantain ice cream. I took the MetroNorth to the last stop on the New Haven line the morning of our meeting, reciting my talking points for the two-hour ride. Exactly five minutes before our two p.m. meeting, I got to his doorstep with my laptop, an ice cream cooler, and a large bag of Kelewele meals. I took a deep breath, rang the doorbell, and said a quick prayer. The gray-haired, middle-aged white man in a casual navy-blue sweater, jeans, and black-rimmed glasses smiled and ushered me inside.

The forest-green hallway adorned with floral artwork flowed into an expansive kitchen and dining room that looked like a disorganized office. Tall stacks of paper, product prototypes, and beverage samples were spread across the countertops and filled the dining chairs. Crates of Honest Tea lined the back wall. The space had a mad-scientist feel to it, and I imagined the kinds of product testing that took place in the room.

"Water, tea . . . anything?" he asked as he put the rest of the

Kelewele menu he'd ordered into the refrigerator. Barry's question interrupted my daydream and snapped me back to reality. "I'm all–all right, thanks," I stuttered, remembering why I was there and what was at stake.

With his back to me as he sorted aluminum containers of plantain lasagna and shepherd's pie into the refrigerator shelves, I took a deep and silent breath. This was my first conversation with a seasoned investor, and I felt like an imposter. I knew Kelewele, but he knew the theory and application of business at full scale. I'd tested my products enough to know that there was a market for them, but even so, it was hard to feel confident. Would he recognize and appreciate the cultural significance of what I was doing? And would it even matter?

I'd grown comfortable pitching the brand to people of color who readily understood the value of plantains as a cross-cultural connector of people and a way to stay rooted in African diasporic identity. But with others, I had to work hard at finding the entry point to make Kelewele relatable to them. Most of those conversations started with a question of some sort: "What's a plantain?" "Plantains are bananas, right?" "Why do you have a rotten banana on display?" (referring to a ripened plantain). What would be my starting point with Barry? I wanted to make the kind of impression that would lead to his investment in Kelewele. But even more so, I wanted to return to my team the next day with good news to share. I wanted the opportunity to tell them that others valued our work and were willing to put their money behind it—a reminder for the hard days that we were building something purposeful that people were excited about and believed in.

On our way to his patio, he stopped to grab a spoon. I acted calm but was shaking as we settled into our seats. Barry arranged the ice cream pints in a line on the table between us and opened them one by one as I pulled up my deck. His silver spoon smoothly sliced through the surface of the creamy Vanilla Ginger pint. He smelled the scoop of ice cream before bringing it to his lips for a taste. "Hmm," was all he said. My eyes were locked on his face as I searched for the slightest expression of interest or disgust. His face remained neutral as he sampled the Moringa Chocolate Chip, Liquid Gold Turmeric, Chocolate Fudge Brownie, and Vanilla Vibranium flavors. His silence threw me off, causing me to fumble through my slides on Kelewele's origin story, financials, and short- and long-term strategies.

He ate, listened, and ate some more before finally giving me his appraisal as he stood up, pacing the length of the gray patio table. Barry liked what he tried but was generous with his critical feedback: He thought my product was niche and lacked an airtight proof of concept that was scalable. "The amount of organic press you've received from *The New York Times* and other notable organizations far outpaces your current operating level. . . . I'd advise you to not give up whatever it is you're doing in your PhD program to pursue this. Is there a lot of interest in plantain products right now? I don't think so. There's no *urgent* need to build this," he reasoned. He encouraged me to keep at it, refine my technical skills, and develop an attractive financial model that could rival that of large-scale vegan ice cream competitors like Van Leewuen, Oatly, and NadaMoo!

I was crushed, even though I knew I had plenty of work still to do in developing the business. Growing my startup in a competitive capitalist landscape would require constant iteration on even my best ideas. I was disappointed that our meeting hadn't gone the way I'd hoped it would, given the work I'd put in, but the rejection was a sobering reminder that practices of Black

Capitalism are complicated and part of a much larger system. Black Capitalists can have the smarts, preparation, and desire to participate in the economic system, but resilience, stamina, and ingenuity are what's needed to have a fighting chance at overcoming the enduring structural challenges that make a relationship to capitalism uniquely different for Black people.

I'm hustling to build a business not because it's sexy or easy (trust me, it's neither), but because I believe in the value and social good it can bring to our interconnected world. As a Black woman, I know uniquely what money can and cannot provide, but in the case of entrepreneurship, using the tools of capitalism to create and own the means of production and capital unlocks access to the power to determine labor practices, business ownership, and environmental and social mandates that can transform people's life chances and choices. My practice of capitalism connects to someone else's practice and so on and so forth.

When we move with this understanding and our North Star is collective economic security, the elusive dream to create sustainable social good within a global capitalist system becomes a bit more attainable. The good news is that this version of capitalism is one that Black people have already built and can serve as the blueprint for us all. It's a model that ensures that thriving is possible despite the structures that deny it for so many.

So how can one thrive in capitalism with an ethical mindset? Well, for starters, it's not about being Jeff Bezos rich. And it's not about hoarding money or shirking one's responsibility to the greater good by avoiding paying taxes. It's about positioning yourself to receive *and* share resources so that you don't have to operate from a place of fear or lack. When you're less afraid and free from a scarcity mindset, you operate from a place of giving and generosity because an abundant mentality unlocks the belief that selflessness creates greater collective security and comfort.

At every rung of the global, Black socioeconomic ladder, there is a hustle to obtain economic security. Each level looks different, but every hustle (hustling for survival, soft living, luxurious living, or professional recognition) is inherently tied to an engagement with the capitalist system in which we operate and that Black people, historically, have had to force their way into ever since emancipation. You can be an Amazon delivery worker by day, an Uber driver by night, and a dog walker somewhere in between. You can be the professional at a toxic hedge fund on Wall Street who sticks around for the yearly bonus while nurturing your side hustle with hopes to turn it into a full-time career. Or you can be the top executive who "made it"—you don't *earn* money anymore, you just *get* it—but who is held accountable by others and critiqued for how you spend your capital and with whom. Or maybe you're the hair braider who's also a house cleaner, market woman, and full-time mother. Or the barbershop owner who can give someone the flyest fade by day and change someone's car oil for less than the Jiffy Lube fee by night, and source a buyer for that exclusive pair of Jordans if the price is right. The list goes on, but no matter the hustle type or level, every practice of hustling is a practice of capitalism, and that makes all of us responsible for a system that we did not create but that we sustain through our everyday actions.

How we participate in the political economy is up to us. Rather than assign the issues of capitalism to "the system" or "the man" while simultaneously reaping whatever benefits we can extract from it, let's dig into the problems and contradictions in which we are deeply entangled. Calling our daily capitalist practices for what they are—capitalist—shifts our collective mindset about who gets to own the means to capital, allows us to build strategies to reappropriate the tools of capitalism to service social good, and makes room for us to get comfortable with the idea and reality that it's okay—in fact, necessary—for Black people to thrive, too. Black Capitalism, as I define it, is about individual transformation being tied to the collective.

Perhaps because Black people have had to force our way into a broken system, we both recognize and embody the contradictions that surround it. It's not that Black Capitalism isn't a contradiction—just the opposite. And so is America. The land of the free, where the phrase "life, liberty, and the pursuit of happiness" is constituted as a promise that has never held true for Black people. In return, Black people have become masters of living in contradiction, in twoness, and the dissonance of it all. Black thriving—*life, liberty, and the pursuit of happiness*—demands we opt into contradictory tensions to break out of the margins we've been relegated to and take up space at the center of a system built by us but not for us.

My relationship to capitalism today is not the one I had when I lived in my mother's house. The arc of my journey in understanding and moving through our economic system has been a nonlinear transition from fear to freedom. In moments where I've been fearful about my financial future and wary about the minute role I play in our massive political economy, I've adopted a scarcity mindset overcome by the pressure to work as hard as possible to desperately hold on to whatever resources I could. But no matter what I did, I couldn't shake the feeling that securing financial stability on my own was not a guarantee. I often felt powerless, disconnected from others, and ill-equipped to create the change I wanted to see. Shifting to an abundance mindset—the belief that there are enough resources for everyone—made the difference in how I think and behave. It allows me to think about my role in capitalism from a position of agency and believe that thriving and financial freedom are not only possible, but also that I and everyone else deserve them too. By centering community and implementing a strategy for how to be *in* but not *of* capitalism, I've learned that there's another way to make sense of capitalism and focus on what it can do *for* us, instead of *to* us.

To opt in to a system so oppressive for Black people, I've had to find ways to use other people's money to do good, break the cycle of poverty that my mother was thrust into, and manifest the life I desire. The road from fear to freedom is nonlinear because our position in capitalism is always changing. The titles that shape our economic position—business owner, student, working professional, unemployed person, gig worker, or somewhere in between—are never permanent. And so how we express our relationship to, and feelings about, capitalism is constantly evolving to meet us where we are and where we strive to be.

CHAPTER 6

A Time After Black?

O. J. SIMPSON: "I'm not Black, I'm O.J."[1]
JAY-Z: "O.J. like, 'I'm not Black I'm O.J.' . . . Okay."[2]

I became fascinated by Orenthal James Simpson's relationship to race in my early graduate school days. The year was 2017 and I was a student in Professor Daphne Brooks's Racial Formations seminar. We were tasked with watching and responding to Yale alum Ezra Edelman's *O.J.: Made in America,* a five-part documentary. Growing up, I had heard the famous line "If the glove doesn't fit, you must acquit"[3] and knew of my mom's admiration for Johnny Cochran, endearingly called "Black America's lawyer," but I knew little about Simpson himself.

The film captures the rise and fall of Simpson's fame against the backdrop of global protest movements and the violent race relations and police brutality that infected Los Angeles between the 1960s and 1990s. I was most intrigued by Simpson's entry, exit, and ultimate return to Blackness. Simpson's famous claim

"I'm not Black, I'm O.J.," made at the height of his career, is both problematic and provocative. For Simpson, to be O.J. but not Black is a permutation of Martin Luther King Jr.'s dream: to be judged *not* by the color of one's skin, but by the content of one's character. The implied hope is that a person can be the subject of their own narrative rather than the racialized object of another's. Many revere MLK for his dream but ridicule Simpson for his declaration. Why? In his book *Representation*, Stuart Hall argues, "What unsettles culture is 'matter out of place'—the breaking of our unwritten rules and codes. . . . What we do with 'matter out of place' is to sweep it up, throw it out, restore the place to order, [and] bring back the normal state of affairs."[4] "Matter out of place" can look like a Black man's attempt to claim his humanity in a white world that rejects his pursuit of freedom. As a result, majority and minority racial groups are in a constant fight for the power of representation—to mark, assign, and classify meaning onto racial identity.

The self-determination of Simpson's claim is both unsettling and aspirational. His individualism painfully dismissed the long history of Black resistance that made it possible for Simpson to enter the historically white spaces that produced his success, and ignored the entrenched social structures that, for many, render his claim ludicrous. But the ridiculousness is what makes it daringly aspirational. Defining who he was on his own terms is an act of agency, even if the social conditions, then and now, render it ignorant or irresponsible. His assertion made in the present tense (what I am versus what I am not) creates room to imagine future states of individual and collective identity.

In America, we've moved from *nigger* to *colored* to *Negro* to *African American* to *Black* in our classification of African descendants. What will come next and who will decide that?

Simpson's claim compels us to consider what post-Blackness can mean.

But what does Simpson have to do with Black Capitalists? As it turns out, a lot. The more people I talked with, read about, or watched on television and film, the more aware I became of desires for self-determination that are divorced from one's racial identity. But certainly not all Black Capitalists, cultural icons, or fictional characters I studied see benefit in disavowing their racial identity. Many proudly identify as Black and credit their racial identity for the way they navigate and make meaning of the world. I don't adjudicate a person's choice. What matters is *why* and *how* those choices are made and their impact on the spaces Black Capitalists occupy. Tracking the core desires, processes, and outcomes that support individual choices allows us to locate gaps between what people aspire to achieve for themselves and what society allows them to obtain.

Born in the summer of 1947 in San Francisco, Simpson grew up in the Potrero Hill housing projects. He once recalled, "Growing up in the ghetto, one of the things I wanted most was not money, but fame, I wanted to be known."[5] His tenure as a running back for the University of Southern California's football team in the late 1960s produced the fame he yearned for and earned him a diverse following as he entered the NFL during a time of racial unrest in the United States.

With the Black Power movement in full swing, many prominent Black athletes boycotted sports to shine a light on the racism that existed in the industry. While others retired their cleats for the cause, Simpson took to the field branding himself as the "counterrevolutionary athlete."[6] He penned a letter to a journalist about his responsibility (or lack thereof) to the Black community: "I strive to be a man first. . . . The negro is always identified with poverty. . . . What I'm doing is not for principles or Black people. No, I'm dealing first with O. J. Simpson, his wife, and his babies."[7] Simpson would go on to tell others who questioned his politics and urged him to protest, "I want to be judged by the content of my character and the caliber of my competence. Don't tell me I gotta do this because I'm Black. . . . I'm not Black, I'm O.J."[8]

And to many of Simpson's white friends, business partners, and associates, he was "colorless." Following continued pressure to be a voice for the Black community, Simpson explained in a publicly broadcast interview how his approach to race shaped his professional career, both on and off the field. His words showcase his self-determination: "I rebel against images because people tend to expect things from you. I created an image by being me. When I get in these arguments with people of the Black community, I say, hey, I've accepted Jesus Christ and I try to do unto others as I would have them do unto me and hey, after that my life is mine. I do what is right and morally acceptable to me. I am not prejudiced in any form. Obviously, I have a white girlfriend."[9]

Given that he was born into poverty, Simpson's choice to assimilate with white culture was not only rational but also a ticket into the life he once dreamed of. His focus on self at the expense of the Black community challenged enduring social norms. And that's the core tension. Simpson's self-identification was both opposed to and aligned with how racial subsets of society identified him, on his behalf. The Black community that Simpson betrayed during the height of his career made a mockery of his racial disavowal. Meanwhile, his elite white social circle viewed Simpson as colorless. Wealth and fame allowed Simpson to create a world where he decided who he was with no material consequence.

Simpson's story can seem exceptional because of its dramatic twists and turns. The highly contentious murder trial, in which he was found not guilty of the murder of his second wife, Nicole Brown Simpson, a rich white woman, led to his fall from fame and favor with his white friends, and consequently, his embrace of a Black identity in search of community. But the existence of his identity politics decades before any questions concerning his criminality mirrors the way some Black people position themselves socially and professionally today. If we set aside the history of global Black protest movements that prioritize community uplift, we can appreciate the self-serving desires of a man to *just be,* untethered to a racial identity designed to cast limitations on who, what, and how one can be in the world.

But regardless of how ideal self-determination may seem, we must account for the systemic social norms that so often prevent it for Black people. Grappling with this contradiction exposes the complicated space between individual agency and rigid social constructions that Black people navigate every day.

In "The Story of O.J.," a track on his 2017 album *4:44,* Jay-Z makes a facetious response to Simpson's racial disavowal. He raps that rigid racial categories are inescapable no matter who you are. But self-fashioning, rooted in economic advancement, is still attainable. As the lyrics go:

> *Light nigga, dark nigga, faux nigga, real nigga*
> *Rich nigga, poor nigga, house nigga, field nigga*
> *Still nigga, still nigga*
> *O.J. like, "I'm not Black, I'm O.J." . . . Okay*[10]

Jay-Z challenges Simpson's identity politics with the argument that no matter one's physical complexion or economic position, Blackness is permanent. The sarcasm laced in Jay-Z's response proves just how invalid it is in a racially codified society.

Through his rhymes, Jay-Z educates the Black community on the long-term returns and value of good credit and investing in one's community. Simpson and Jay-Z have different answers to the question of what they owe to the Black community. For Simpson, he's only responsible for the well-being of himself, his wife, and his children. For Jay-Z, he raps "a million dollars' worth of game for $9.99"—a model for collective financial freedom.

Jay-Z's key critique of Simpson is his lack of investment in the Black community. He acknowledges the collective Black struggle for economic liberation and offers a blueprint for advancement. Jay-Z was born into poverty and grew up in the Marcy housing projects of Brooklyn. His trajectory from drug dealer to rapper to billionaire businessman is the quintessential rags-to-riches story. It's equal parts aspirational and exceptional.

When you compare public responses to the two men's identity politics, Simpson is widely criticized for his racial disavowal and assimilation to elite white culture at the expense of the Black community. In contrast, Jay-Z, who racially identifies as Black, ironically is criticized by the Black community in ways that are similar to his critique of Simpson. Jay-Z views himself as a "field nigga" who is down with the cause. But some of his widely publicized business proceedings leave many questioning the authenticity of his commitment to the Black community and his effort to disrupt institutionalized racism.

One deal that flooded news cycles for weeks was the 2019 announcement of the multiyear partnership between Jay-Z's company, Roc Nation, and the National Football League. Through this partnership, Roc Nation took responsibility for leading the NFL's live game entertainment and social justice strategy. The deal also strategically positioned Jay-Z to acquire significant ownership interest in an NFL team, thereby granting him access into the hyper-exclusive billionaire boys' club of national football team owners. While the deal's magnitude alone was newsworthy, what garnered immediate criticism was the timing and Jay-Z's vocal disapproval of past NFL behavior.

A few years prior, Jay-Z had called out the NFL for its handling of former San Francisco 49ers quarterback Colin Kaepernick's 2016 symbolic protest of racial inequality. Many football fans viewed Kaepernick's bended knee during the national anthem as offensive. The act was intended to shed light on the dissonance between the principles of equity and fairness in the anthem lyrics and the gross institutional atrocities endured by Black people at the hands of law enforcement in the United States. Kaepernick refused to be the counterrevolutionary athlete that Simpson was during his football career. In the weeks that followed, Kaepernick was professionally blackballed, and the NFL made no public attempts to support him throughout the backlash.

So when news broke that Jay-Z shook hands with commissioner Roger Goodell of the NFL, the very organization he had criticized for supporting the racist sentiment of its white audience base, public response was swift and largely unkind. When asked about Kaepernick during the official press conference, Jay-Z noted: "For me it's like action, [an] actionable item, what are we gonna do with it? Everyone heard, we hear what you're saying, and everybody knows I agree with what you're saying [in Kaepernick's protest]. So what are we gonna do? You know what I'm saying? Reach millions and millions of people, or we get stuck on Colin not having a job."[11]

Opinion writers affiliated with *The Black Youth Project, USA*

Today, The Guardian, Forbes, The Atlantic, and others called Jay-Z a sellout, a capitalist, or the fallout man for the league's disregard for the concerns of its Black players. As Jemele Hill puts it in her article "Jay-Z Helped the NFL Banish Colin Kaepernick," "Jay-Z has given the NFL exactly what it wanted: guilt free access to black audiences, culture, entertainers, and influencers."[12] Brittani McNeil argued in her *Black Youth Project* article, "We Shouldn't Be Surprised by Jay-Z's NFL Move: He's Always Been a Capitalist and This Is What Capitalism Looks Like": "Capitalism wins again. And again. And again. So why do we keep acting so surprised by it? Why do we keep letting it catch us off guard? Why do we keep excusing it and those with power who continue to uphold it? . . . Even though we know there's very little chance of us mimicking Jay-Z's success within our current systems, many of us still cheer for him when he spouts these ideas."[13]

Hemal Jhaveri adds to this sentiment in her *USA Today* piece "Jay-Z's Partnership with the NFL Is Just Another Reminder That Capitalism Always Wins." Jhaveri contends that "while Jay-Z's intentions may be good, this is about acknowledging the limits of how much progressive movements can achieve when they align themselves with entrenched systems of power."[14]

Others read Jay-Z's NFL deal as consistent with his ongoing practice of capitalism even if entering in this particular deal "blurs the line of culture and commerce by putting a price tag on oppression," as Kori Hale notes in her *Forbes* article "Sorry Kaep: Jay-Z's Commerce and Culture NFL Partnership Failure."[15] Regardless of the social activist bent to Jay-Z's "woke capitalism," it is a capitalism that prioritizes the extraction of surplus value. As Derecka Purnell puts it, Jay-Z is "variably positioned as a quintessential black capitalist: professing that freedom is one's ability to own oneself and acquire wealth," a "billionaire who wants to be an NFL team owner," or a self-proclaimed "socially conscious billionaire."[16]

David Zirin, in his "Jay-Z Isn't a Sellout, He's a Capitalist," puts it frankly: "Jay-Z is a boss. Colin Kaepernick and Eric Reid [fellow NFL player and Kaepernick supporter] are workers. It is the interest of workers in the NFL to unite and say that black-balling people for their political beliefs is never going to be OK. . . . It is in Shawn Carter's interest to stand up for himself. It's not 'millions and millions' who are going to be helped. It's one person."[17] According to Zirin, Jay-Z's focus on *his* bottom line has always been his hustle. "A hustle he told us, over 20 years ago," Zirin adds, "we were never to knock."[18]

The critics did not hold back, but there's something interesting about admonitions to the Black community about buying stories of Black exceptionalism. None of them offer the *possibility* of productive outcomes of the finalized deal or a subversive strategy for Roc Nation to drive change. Public opinion suggests we've resigned ourselves to thinking that *nothing* impactful can come out of the deal. Really? Where is our curiosity about the "action" Jay-Z said himself it's time to focus on? There's accountability in action, and action is a tangible thing we can measure and improve upon. But when we throw our hands up to say no good can come out of this yet tune into the NFL halftime show at Super Bowl parties year after year, that's when the needle stops moving.

Race makes a difference in how we participate in capitalism. Are we asking if Bill Gates, Elon Musk, Jeff Bezos, or the next white billionaire is committed to the Black community and putting up the money to prove it? Is the sellout conversation even a talking point when we consider the business dealings of white elites? There's nothing for them to sell out of. White people are not held to the same intraracial expectation to lift as they climb. At face value, the title of *capitalist* is equal opportunity. But when you're Black (not to mention famous) and own that title, you are held to a different and higher level of scrutiny and expectation. And with that comes the responsibility to participate in capitalism in such a way that yields economic thriving for you and your community.

Capitalism is a dirty game that so many of us don't want to play. But truth be told, we're *all* playing whether we want to or not. So the question becomes, Can you get dirty without being dirty if it means using the tools of capitalism to create new outcomes?

We can't ignore the deeply entrenched systems of inequity that drive free-market capitalism today, but we also must acknowledge the growing number (Jay-Z is not the exception to this) of Black people who grapple with capitalism in ways that should not be reduced to the sellout narrative. Capitalism is complex in its distribution and execution. Someone's racialized relationship to the political economy should not be oversimplified. The hard work we must all do is adopt the mindset of Black Capitalism—and determine how we implement its tactics and strategies in our everyday lives to advance collective thriving.

◆ ◆ ◆

Evidence proves that the Black community can be critical of Black participation in capitalism within the entertainment industry. But what do fictional television portrayals of Black people navigating corporate America tell us about the expectations society places on them when the pressure of fame and stardom is

absent? What are the shifting desires, sacrifices, and internal conflicts that shape the ethics of Black participation in capitalism?
What demands of American capitalism are exclusively delegated
to Black people?

And can we read these fictive depictions as stories of resilience and strategic thinking rather than the reductive sellout
narrative? A look at *Industry*, the HBO British-American television drama, provides an answer by helping us understand the
tax on Blackness within a capitalist identity and the choices a
Black person can feel forced to make in return for a fighting
chance at a new financial future.

It's important to note that none of the portrayals in this
chapter (real or fictive) fully capture my definition of a Black
Capitalist or the practice of Black Capitalism. They fall short in
revealing the potential and real opportunity to create social
good that is attached to Black Capitalist identity as I define it.
But what they do offer is a lens into the tensions and contradictions of being both Black and a capitalist.

Blurring Fiction and Reality

From *The Wolf of Wall Street* to *Succession*, not only do we love
money, we love film and television about money. As entertaining
(and anxiety inducing!) as *Succession* might be, every time I
watched it, I was reminded how the reality of the show's main
characters would change if the people in question were Black.
There were no racial stereotypes for the white characters to con-
tend with. No questions asked about their competence because
of their whiteness. And no financial struggle that either they or
their loved ones were connected to. Life *is* dramatic for these
characters, but not on account of the meaning others place on

their whiteness. All of this changes when the main character is Black, as in *Industry*.

Harper, a young Black woman played by Myha'la Herrold, has no family to rely on, no inherited wealth to inspire the kind of confidence guaranteed wealth can, and certainly no white privilege. Season 1 follows Harper and her cohort of analysts interning at Pierpoint & Company, a premier investment bank in London, as they vie for return offers at the end of their six-month internship.[19]

The first episode opens with short snippets of the interview process as prospective hires awkwardly answer questions posed by hiring managers. Harper's interview is of particular importance. The dialogue between her and her interviewer Eric, a middle-aged Asian Pierpoint executive played by Ken Leung, gives viewers a glimpse into Harper's past life and foreshadows the challenges she will face at Pierpoint.

> ERIC: *(reading Harper's résumé)* Blah, blah, blah, blah, blah. I've never seen anyone put their IQ on a CV before. . . . Why are you here, then?
>
> HARPER: Well, it's not a very political answer, but I think mediocrity is too well hidden by parents who hire private tutors. I am here on my own.
>
> ERIC: Every successful business is full of people who've spent money nurturing unremarkable talent.
>
> HARPER: I think this is the closest thing to meritocracy there is, and I only ever want to be judged on the strength of my abilities.
>
> ERIC: And paid for it.
>
> HARPER: I guess.
>
> ERIC: I didn't realize we recruited from SUNY Binghamton.

HARPER: It's a non-target.

ERIC: You know how many mountains I'd have to move
    to get you to London for good?[20]

As a Black viewer minutes into the episode, I pick up on the
show's commentary on the relationship between class, meritocracy, and the financial industry. And the sobering fact that the
fictional story before my eyes feels eerily real—I see myself in
Harper. Her desire to work at Pierpoint is based on her belief
that no matter where she comes from (a non-target American
university), her intelligence and work ethic matter most in
achieving success at a "meritocratic" place like Pierpoint. She did
not go to any of the finance industry's target recruiting schools
like Harvard, Yale, or Princeton for undergrad. This is the first
of many unique challenges Harper faces. She must compensate
for a perceived lack of intelligence by strategically including her
IQ on her résumé. To prove that despite the classification of her
alma mater as a non-target school (and in effect, *her* as a non-
desirable intern), she is in fact competent. To know and name
in the interview that her alma mater is a non-target school reveals Harper's determination to occupy elite white spaces that
extend beyond the reach of her social pedigree.

Watching the scene took me back to my early days at Goldman Sachs. That Sales and Trading Insight Day I attended when
I first learned the bank was full of the people who were "supposed" to be there—white men who studied finance and economics at Ivy League schools. My name tag announcing my
major, Social and Cultural Analysis, was akin to SUNY Binghamton displayed on Harper's résumé. We weren't textbook re-
cruits. Even though I had attended NYU, which was a target
school for Goldman Sachs at the time, I was still out of place. I

could tell people were wondering, much like Eric, "How did she get here?" And the reality for both Harper and me was that people questioning our presence in "white-only" spaces happened before we were even permitted full entry. We were never afforded the initial belief by others that an investment bank is a place where we *should* be. We would need to prove it.

The scene cuts to Harper in London. She enters an empty trading floor for the first time dressed in a gray blazer and black slacks, a Pierpoint lanyard draped around her neck, and her long black braids tied back in a ponytail. The floor comes alive later that morning as phones ring and people chatter and work from their dual-monitor computer sets. The piece of advice that analysts receive from managing directors and partners during their orientation sessions is: "Make yourselves indispensable."[21] While the analysts are relatively friendly with one another, the air at Pierpoint is thick with competition as interns make overt attempts to outperform one another. They work overtime, sleep at the office to maximize productivity, fulfill team lunch orders, and grovel at the feet of senior leadership.

The intense work conditions are put under a microscope with the death of Hari, an analyst of Southeast Asian descent. He dies in one of the employee washrooms after a string of sleepless nights that culminates in an all-nighter to ensure the completion of a pitch deck for a morning review with his manager. Noticing a minor font error after releasing the deck to the printing department for a nine a.m. client meeting, Hari cracks under the pressure. Too scared to tell his manager about the mishap, he sequesters himself in a bathroom stall. Hunched over a toilet, he slowly rocks his body back and forth as he goes through the emotional roller coaster of a panic attack. Yelling about the "fucking amateur" mistake and uttering a few words in Urdu on the phone about the font needing to be "Helvetica 12," he looks to the right and left of the bare walls that enclose him. He looks up as his eyelids pull back making the white of his eyes eerily large as he slowly sinks onto the floor.[22]

Robert, the stereotypical white male analyst more interested in partying than working, inadvertently finds Hari when he sees two legs clothed in navy-blue slacks and shiny black shoes laid out at the base of the wooden bathroom stall door. The visual of police officers and emergency personnel pushing Hari away in a black body bag on a mortuary trolley creates an office spectacle. Management attempts to mitigate the reputational risk by quickly convening the analyst cohort into a dimly lit gray conference room, warning the visibly distressed interns to avoid all communication with the press. Watching this, one might think: "This is fiction. A ploy to add dramatic effect to the storyline."

My reading of Hari's death was quite the opposite. Two years prior to my internship at Goldman Sachs, the story of Bank of America intern Moritz Erhardt made global news. After working three nights straight to meet the demands of his job, Erhardt was found dead in his London flat.[23] He was twenty-one years old. Two years later, news would break of twenty-two-year-old Sarvshreshth Gupta's death. He was a Goldman Sachs analyst based in San Francisco. Though Gupta's death was ruled a suicide, it is believed the arduous work hours and pressure to deliver were what killed him.[24] The day of his death Gupta made a call to his father recounting how he hadn't slept for days due to pressing client meetings, deck presentations, and a demanding manager. Within a few hours of that call, he was dead.[25] Sadly, Erhardt's and Gupta's stories aren't exceptional. There are other accounts of healthy young people who have died in connection to toxic working conditions in the finance industry. The risk of one's physical well-being presents yet another real challenge that must be overcome. And when you have something to prove that others don't, the risk is heightened.

In *Industry,* the scene then cuts to the women's restroom where two white-passing interns, Maeve and Yasmin, linger by the sinks talking between themselves about the disturbing incident.

MAEVE: Apparently he just fucking died.

YASMIN: It's fucking scary.

MAEVE: Lesson is, don't hire people who really need the job.

YASMIN: What does that mean?

MAEVE: I mean, certain types of people feel the need to overcompensate because they feel inadequate. It's also bad for us.

YASMIN: How do you mean?

MAEVE: Take the girl with the nose ring. It's impossible to compete with this girl's narrative. I mean, everything's aligned for her.

YASMIN: You know nothing about her.

MAEVE: Well, I know she went to a shit uni, and I know she's Black. And I know those things are mutually exclusive, sure, but together . . . tick, tick.

YASMIN: You are fucking vile.

MAEVE: *(laughs)* Oh, come on. It's just . . . realistic.[26]

Immediately following the exchange, Harper exits one of the bathroom stalls, leaving the women dumbfounded and embarrassed. Maeve awkwardly exits the bathroom, avoiding eye contact with Harper, while Yasmin apologizes to Harper, who remains silent and stoic throughout the encounter. What is viscerally relatable about this moment are all the ways I and others are forced to deal with micro- and macroaggressions aimed to justify how it is Black people made it into corporate America (or anywhere white people can be found).

"You're so eloquent!" Tick. "You bring so much diversity to the table!" Tick. "Are you from the inner city?" Tick. These comments are just a few of the indirect ways white people have broached the topic with me as I've sat silent—knowing they never said the same to my white counterparts. What Maeve calls "realistic" in a fit of laughter is actually racist and puts Harper in a compromising situation where she's forced to pick her battles. She can put the white woman on notice, adding fuel to her fire, or disengage and sit with the reality that her peers view her as a quota check. The options create a lose-lose situation that presents another obstacle for Harper to tackle. She, like so many real-life Black professionals, must push through the psychological trauma of not belonging to get what she came for: financial freedom.

The episode concludes with Harper's execution of her first major client trade. Eric, the Asian executive who hired her and is now her manager, shakes her hand upon completion of the trade and says, "Now I see you." Then immediately asks, "Why is there a ring in your nose? You cattle?" to which she quietly smirks.[27] Harper rewards herself for her earned visibility by booking a lavish hotel for the night instead of going home to the now-empty apartment she once shared with Hari. In a plush white bathrobe with the London cityscape behind her, Harper takes a selfie eating a juicy burger and uploads the picture to a Pierpoint drive reserved for uploading official university transcripts. This brazen act casts doubt on whether Harper actually graduated from SUNY Binghamton. We find out later that she never did.

In the episodes that follow, Harper's perspective on money and how her past informs her present desire for wealth unfold. Episode 2's plotline is centered on Harper's hunt to find a new apartment and a new roommate. During her lunch hour she tours an open listing where she meets with a young white man named Jacob who is subletting the room. Sitting together in Jacob's living room, the two roll a blunt, drink wine, and get to know each other. Inevitably, the conversation turns to Harper's source of income, which makes for a charged exchange between the two strangers.

> JACOB: What do you do?
> HARPER: I'm in sales. For a bank . . . Pierpoint.
> JACOB: Isn't that where that guy died?
> *(a long silent pause)*
> JACOB: How do you sleep at night?
> HARPER: What's that mean?
> JACOB: I mean *(scoffs)* you know.
> HARPER: No, I don't. You're gonna have to tell me.
> JACOB: Bankers. That level of self-interest is just toxic, isn't it?
> HARPER: That's kind of reductive.
> JACOB: But isn't it a bit gauche to judge success with money?
> HARPER: Not if you've never had any. *(swigs her last bit of wine, grabs her jacket, and walks out)*[28]

"Louder, Harper!" I thought to myself as I watched this tense exchange for the first time. I was empathetic to Harper because, again, as a Black woman I've actually been there. Judged by others and forced to justify my choices to people with fixed perceptions of capitalism and my participation within it. Harper's prospective landlord renders her choice inhumane while, in fact, her humanity is on full display. Jacob knows nothing about her, where she's come from, or the hurdles she's jumped to even work at Pierpoint. He projects his ethics onto her as if his lived experience is the norm. Who is to adjudicate Harper's decision to work at Pierpoint because of the lack of resources she's had access to? Apparently, a privileged white man. In an act of dignity, Harper cuts the conversation short, but the reality is that for so many of us, we get guilt-tripped and caught in the cycle of explaining to others why it is we desire to thrive.

The past Harper alludes to comes to the fore when Teddy, her ex-boyfriend, travels to London for a visit. They rehash the conditions that led to their breakup during college, enjoy passionate sex, and take comfort in each other's company. That is, until Harper learns that Teddy stole an embroidered fleece jacket from one of her Pierpoint clients during a night out. Teddy flaunts the pilfered garment, making light of the situation and expecting Harper to do the same. She doesn't. Enraged and panicked, Harper yells at her ex for stealing from "her clients" as she weighs the cost of Teddy's actions. He mocks her for referring to rich white people as "her clients" and using her "white voice" on him. This only angers Harper more, landing Teddy and his belongings on the curb. The late-night scene ends with Teddy walking away into the distance saying, "Should have never gave y'all niggas money."[29]

Teddy and Harper's exchange represents the real tension

often created when Black people get access to money in historically white spaces while the people close to them do not. Survival behaviors, like code-switching and cultural assimilation, employed in the workplace can seep into one's personal life and rupture one's sense of community. The closer one gets to financial freedom, the harder it can be to preserve relationships with people who do not have the same opportunities to also shift their economic position and adopt new ways of living when access to money isn't a concern. The potential disconnect between people is further complicated by the fact that many Black people are responsible for lifting as they climb the economic ladder—regardless of the isolation they may feel in the process. There's an expectation to carry the financial burden as the one who "made it"—even if people treat you differently because of it. The desire to thrive has its costs.

The season is punctuated by episode 4, when Harper goes rogue trying to make a lucrative return on a trade that she mishandles, jeopardizing her employment at Pierpoint. Terrified by the thought of telling Eric that she bought more shares of stock than requested by a client, Harper attempts to manipulate and even beg the operations lead in the middle office to grant her time to correct the error before flagging the issue himself. With the clock winding down to the close of the trading day, Harper leaves the office to meet with a trusted client. Her intention is to persuade the client to buy into a trade idea that will offset the loss incurred by her error. The effort is useless. The client rejects the idea and warns Harper to come clean to maintain her dignity. A tearful and defeated Harper breaks down with no option but to tell Eric the truth.

I felt defeated watching this scene. Why? Because as a Black woman eager to see another Black woman win in an arena where we so often lose in pay, promotion, and visibility, I was convinced her negligent actions would get her fired. Harper's attempt to cover up her mistake speaks to the fact that Black professionals are often held to a higher standard of performance and scrutiny. One mistake can erase the positive impact of weeks' worth of excellent work and create irrevocable doubt in one's credibility and competence. Many believe that how someone does *one* thing is how they do *everything*. But grace is often extended for the incompetence of unimpressive white people when they have money and a powerful social network. As Eric affirmed in his interview with Harper: "Every successful business is full of people who've spent money nurturing unremarkable talent." But as the Black recruit without wealth or pedigree in a largely white, elite organization, Harper must be perfect to prove her worth, or at the very least, create the false perception of perfection. I know the feeling because I've been in corporate spaces that felt psychologically unsafe and wondered, "How can I grow without fear of how my mistakes will be used against me?" Management always placed me in performance quartiles to measure my value against my peers, and like Harper, I felt that winning the competition was not the only thing I had to worry about.

Harper's first deal earned Eric's respect, and another one would elevate her standing among her peers. Her ambition, though admirable, was rooted in fear. The urgent need to outperform drove her to make poor choices. What sets Harper apart is that her peers who come from wealth don't operate with the same level of intensity and desperation. They don't have to, as their self-worth is not up for debate. Though her peers *want* the return offer, they don't *need* it. The internship is just a job to them, but for Harper it's a rare opportunity to start a new life. For many Black professionals who relate to Harper (myself included), the gravity of what is at stake produces a tremendous amount of pressure, especially when compounded with other challenges that are unique to a Black identity.

The workday ends with Harper and Eric standing in the rain as she confesses her misbooked trade. In return, Eric shares his discovery of her nonexistent transcript after calling the admissions office at SUNY Binghamton. The revelation makes her the most underqualified analyst he has ever hired. Harper's termination seems imminent, but instead Eric says: "People like us. Born at the bottom. Where would you put our percentage chance of ever making that top quintile? It's about 3 percent. That's intimidating. We intimidate people here. Why is that? Because hunger is not a birthright. Your qualifications don't have to be a problem for you. Because they don't have to be a problem for me. You understand what I'm saying?"[30]

Mic drop. It appears Eric is speaking to Harper, but that's not the case. He is addressing *all* Black people—fictive *and* real. In a few short words he names the inheritance reserved for the minority: white fear. Scarcity and a survival mentality are not a birthright. But when Black people choose to act on this belief as an expression of their own humanity, the privilege white people have inherited for centuries is jeopardized, triggering feelings of scarcity and survival mentality in their own lives. When I catch people's surprise at the sole Black woman—me—in a business meeting, or insecurity hearing all that I've worked for, or worrisome stares at me and friends gallivanting in the Hamptons, I'm reminded that for some, my mere presence checks their subconscious belief that abundance and thriving equates to whiteness.

For Simpson and Jay-Z, I've challenged us to reconsider the exceptionalism we often ascribe to their stories. But as for Eric's response to Harper's omission and her invalid transcript, that is an exceptional case. Eric is an Asian man who was born at the bottom yet somehow breaks into the 3 percent. He wields his corporate power to absolve the analyst with the least impressive résumé of her wrongdoing because he sees a part of himself in her, gritty, tenacious, and persistent. Eric chooses to do what white people often do for their white buddies in corporate spaces—cut them some slack. Although I was relieved to observe this rare act of compassion, I wondered: What if her manager had been white? Would they, like Eric, know the words to speak to Harper's mental state or understand the rationale driving her choices? If not, would they seek understanding or rely on assumptions based on stereotypes of Black people? Would they value her humanity over her imperfection? And would recognition of Harper's experience even matter? Maybe. What if the manager had been Amy Cooper, the unsuspecting liberal white woman who was a portfolio manager, yet in her private life lied to police about a Black man threatening her life during a midday walk in NYC's Central Park? What hidden white fear or hate could Harper have been the victim of? I don't know. But my uncertainty about how this moment would have ended for her, or for me had I been in Harper's shoes, is the point.

Despite Eric's show of racial and class solidarity, which keeps Harper employed, the remaining episodes unravel a dramatic turn of events, in which senior women leaders conspire to push Eric out of Pierpoint. Caught in the middle of the oust as Eric's analyst, Harper angles to preserve her place at the firm by siding with whoever has the upper hand at any point in time. Daria, one of the white women who puppeteers Eric's exit, catches on to Harper's tactics, which tarnishes their relationship. It leaves Harper fearing that her chance of receiving a full-time offer are next to none. With her confidence bruised and paralyzed by paranoia, Harper flunks her final presentation—the last opportunity analysts have to impress senior leadership and vie for a return offer. Her twenty-minute speech and Q&A session, which is broadcast on screens across the trading floor, is cut short as she suffers a panic attack, falls speechless, and flees the conference room to the main-floor lobby, where she is comforted by her Ghanaian colleague—the only other Black analyst in her cohort.

Surprisingly, and what Harper does not see, is that back in the conference room Daria defends Harper despite her pitiful presentation. She assures senior leaders of Harper's work ethic and ability to put the job before herself at all costs. Daria makes a convincing argument on Harper's behalf, but the hiring committee's final decision remains unknown as the scene ends. Business proceeds as usual throughout the day as analysts anxiously await the evening phone call from the management team to tell them their fate. Sitting at her desk and staring at the time and her landline phone, Harper finally gets *the* call. Watching the tense moment brought back to memory the time I was sitting at the help desk at my work-study job at NYU's Avery Fisher Center and got the call from Goldman Sachs that would shift the trajectory of my own career.

Viewers are left wondering about Harper's fate as we expect to hear Daria's voice when Harper picks up the phone. But instead, the scene cuts to Harper sitting at a dining table with Eric, who was ousted weeks before because of a coup led by Daria to usurp male power. They are joined by Adler, the head of the de-

partment. Adler incentivizes Harper to retract an earlier statement she made accusing Eric for harassment while under his
employ, which aided his resignation. He communicates to
Harper Eric's indispensability to Pierpoint and the unrecoup-
able damage to the firm if Eric took his clients to a competing
bank.

What's significant here is that Harper is presented with the
single most important decision of her career, which will dictate
her financial future. She chooses to retract her statement—Eric
is reinstated, Daria is terminated, and most important, she's guaranteed the return offer. Yasmin, the wealthy heiress who is
Harper's new roommate, confronts Harper on Daria's exit and
Eric's reentry, resulting in an argument between the two women.
Harper attempts to defend her role in the drama by labeling Yasmin clueless about "having to live for two fucking people," to
which Yasmin coldly responds, "You play broken well, but you're
really just a cunt."[31]

Viewing the scene made me wonder: Is it that Harper *plays*
broken well, or does Yasmin perceive Harper *as* broken because
of her own position of wealth and her inability to relate to Harper's lived experience? I thought that had Yasmin been in Harper's shoes, it's likely she would have had the wherewithal to
withstand any retaliation due to her family's royalty and the potential revenue they could generate for the firm. Yasmin could
afford to rally behind a gendered power struggle because she
didn't have to worry about having enough money to support
herself—for the rest of her life.

What Yasmin reads as "cunt" behavior, I read as acts of self-
preservation. Make no mistake, the incessant lying, manipula-
tion, and politicking *is* toxic both on-screen and in some of
the organizations I've been a part of. But that doesn't change

the fact that problematic corporate cultures exist today and will continue to, at least for now. People like Harper and myself are sometimes presented with difficult ethical choices where doing the right thing or advocating for oneself doesn't always pay off, literally. There's a trade-off when what's at stake is a shot at financial freedom. Again, the point is not to judge personal choices, but rather to understand *why* certain choices are made and not others, and to appreciate the fact that though people can be presented with the same set of choices, like Harper and Yasmin, the risk attached to a choice can vary based on who you are, which has everything to do with the choices you then make. Knowing this teaches us so much more about the condition of people, and the steps we can take to change it for the better, than a value judgment ever could.

◆　◆　◆

Industry's plotline complicates fictive portrayals of Black participation in capitalism, as well as Simpson and Jay-Z's identity politics. Because Harper is the principal character, viewers are compelled to track her progression throughout her internship and the obstacles that lie between her and the return offer. Harper moves through Pierpoint in survival mode as if she is *in* but not *of* the firm. Never resting on her laurels or allowing herself to get inculcated in the culture like those around her, she is critical of the firm and its employees, yet she can make a moral case for capitalism (as she claims to have done in an eight-thousand-word college paper). She demonstrates adeptness in handling microaggressions with calculated composure and competing with people who view her as a threat because she "checks the boxes" of a diverse hire. These tactics mirror that of Wall Street's under-commons.

Harper is expected to buckle given the pressure she shoulders on account of a toxic work culture, nurtured paranoia, and imposter syndrome looming large over her. But instead, she proves her indispensable value to the firm—throwing up a metaphorical middle finger to Pierpoint. The joke is on them for hiring someone who simultaneously is the least qualified hire and yet the firm's most promising and effective analyst. Regardless of Harper's methods, Black people watching her victory, including me, can take comfort in the reminder that hunger should not be the expectation for the Black lived experience.

The sellout narrative in *Industry* is complicated and emotionally charged. As we learned in *Black Monday,* its two common thematic options—assimilate and gain continued access to the life of the rich and powerful or lose it all—do not map onto Harper's story and her position as a young adult. She is not driven by desires to amass copious wealth, but rather by a need to maintain her new economic position and not regress to her former one.

A belief system emerges in the process: The opportunity for Black thriving should be a birthright. But Harper's story mirrors how race and class can change one's inheritance and trajectory at birth, and consequently, one's ability to realize these elusive American ideals as a Black person. The focus on Black thriving is urgent and dismantles public opinions about what Black people are entitled to in relation to white people.

While subtle, the difference in motivation between the main characters in *Black Monday* and *Industry* is significant. Working at Pierpoint and employing the tactics needed to do so is not predicated on an egotistical power trip to be rich, but rather on a rational fear of being poor, again. Harper's rationale reads a lot like Dennis's from the undercommons. Choosing to stay at Goldman Sachs is a better bet than going back to what and where he came from. So when Simpson, having grown up in the ghetto, talks about needing to protect his financial position, or when Jay-Z raps that "financial freedom [is] my only hope" after years of hustling street corners in the projects, the importance of financial freedom in Harper's fictional story also holds true in the real world. And it resonates with the real lives of Black Capitalists in Wall Street's undercommons, the transatlantic financial circuit, the global gig economy, and the many spaces where Black Capitalism is at work today.

These fictional portrayals and real-life examples suggest that the motives for one's intentional participation in capitalism shouldn't be reduced to the central harms capitalism often produces: resource hoarding, labor exploitation, and surplus capital extraction at any cost. A person's *life chances,* like their race and economic position, can play an informative role in their *life choices* to occupy contentious spaces, especially if doing so produces a level of financial freedom and collective thriving otherwise unknown.

Art imitates life and vice versa. Popular culture, television, and film teach us so much yet leave much to be desired. They show us how Blackness makes a difference in how people can be perceived in the political economy and what they do about it. They also teach us about the inescapability of Blackness. And yet they fall short in depicting the possibility for social good or the transformative potential of a Black Capitalist identity. Perhaps the limited nuance in these depictions imitates our own struggle to imagine Black Capitalism as more than a contradiction. No matter the level of success, wealth, or fame we achieve, a reckoning with our Blackness is always present, which challenges us to reconstruct our understanding of Black life within the economy by studying a blueprint for capitalism, built by Black people, that points us toward collective social good.

CHAPTER 7

Rebuilding the House

Who knew that just five years after my college graduation from NYU I'd come back. But this time as an adjunct professor at the Stern School of Business. On the first day of the fall semester, I walked into my classroom to find fifteen fresh-faced first-year students who had registered for my Commerce and Culture class. For the next fourteen weeks we met twice a week to discuss economic theories and the connections among business, society, and government, and its impact on the world. My intention for my students was twofold: Develop their analytical writing skills, and most important, challenge them to think critically about social phenomena and their role within it. The student who challenged me the most was Vinny, an eighteen-year-old Italian "cool kid" who had contagious charisma and made a habit of turning assignments in late. A couple weeks into the course, the class was having a spirited debate about labor violations in corporate America when Vinny's hand shot up from the front of the room. "A lot of the social problems we read about and see are sad, but I just don't get how we can change any of it," he said.

"Hm, I see. So tell me—why are you here, Vinny?" I responded.

"What do you mean?"

"I mean, why are you *here,* at Stern Business School," I said.

"Oh . . . honestly?" Vinny asked.

"Yes, honestly! Let's explore this. Why are you here, Vinny?"

"Don't judge me, but honestly . . . because I want a finance job where I can make a lot of money," he said.

"Okay. Why else?" I probed.

"That's it."

"And why is *that*?" I asked while his classmates listened intently.

"Because I don't have any power to change anything," Vinny replied.

"You're not alone in thinking this way, Vinny. But the good news is that this idea is not true. It's my hope that by the end of the semester, you'll have reason to believe me," I said.

For the weeks thereafter, my students would analyze global stories of social, political, and economic resistance to the harms of capitalism that challenge the status quo and provide practical solutions for creating a new way of being, and in turn, a new kind of economic system that values people first, not output. On the last day of class I led my students in a reflective conversation, prompting them to consider the biggest takeaways from the semester and what ideas they would carry with them long after our class was over. The group discussion veered toward recalling one of my lectures that explored what the etymology of *economics,* the household, power, and the "master's house" all have to do with one another. Vinny's remarks during our final conversation would become my own greatest takeaway from teaching.

The word *economics* is derived from the Greek word *oikos,* meaning "household" or "family." In Aristotle's *Economics,* he broadens the definition to include the management of finances within the household, the roles people play (like farming, cleaning, hiring labor, and guarding property) to keep up the home, and the power dynamics between people who dictate how the home is maintained.[1] Not only is the household the root of any society, it's also the building block for economics as we know it. But all of this can sound a bit esoteric and abstract. So I asked my students a question to connect the dots between Aristotle's theory of the household and Audre Lorde's critique of the master's house. "For those of you who live here at NYU and have made it your home away from home, how do you like it?" I asked. Their responses were mostly positive as they cited "friends," "social groups," "community," and "a good education" as reasons for liking the house they live in.

"But NYU also gets criticized a lot," one of my quieter students chimed in. "It's a real estate juggernaut—the largest in the city. And it's super expensive, which makes it hard for a lot of people to be here. That's why I commute because I can't afford to live here," she said, which silenced her peers who were prone to debate.

"Okay. So when we consider the critiques of *this* house, or any of the other institutions we've studied, what are the tools of capitalism that are used to manage the house?" I asked.

"Exploitation," "greed," and "exclusion" were some of the answers. But before I could follow up with another question, Vinny interjected: "But there are also tools that can be used for good, right?"

I struggled to contain my smile and excitement. "Yes! Yes! Now here's a big question for you. Can using any of *those* tools—like creativity and resilience and others that are not inherently harmful—in new ways change the house you occupy for the better?" I asked.

My hope for Vinny came true by what he said in response: "As a collective . . . *possibly.*"

"Yes, Vinny. And 'possibly' is more than enough reason to try."

◆ ◆ ◆

The tools of capitalism used by Black Capitalists include social, cultural, and financial capital; creativity; ingenuity; resilience; and a competitive spirit. One example of this is homeowners Paul and Tenisha Austin's story of two appraisals. The Black couple, based in California, bought a home ten minutes north of San Francisco for $550,000 in 2016.[2] Soon thereafter the Austins went to work on renovating their home. In an initial mortgage refinance application, the home was appraised for $1,450,000. Less than a year later, when the Austins decided to refinance their mortgage to fund major enhancements to the property, their lender hired Janette Miller, a white woman, to appraise the home. Miller valued the property at $995,000, which was $455,000 less than what it was worth just months prior. Shocked but not discouraged, the Austins did two things. First, they demanded the lender have another appraiser provide a second opinion. And second, they "whitewashed" their home. On the day of the appraisal, the Austins removed all evidence that a Black family lived in the home. They swapped places with a white female friend who fronted as the homeowner and showed her family photos, instead of the Austins', to the new appraiser.

Unsurprisingly, the new appraiser valued the Austins' home at $1,482,500—almost half a million dollars more than Miller's valuation. The Austins used the tools of capitalism to game the system upon realizing the monetary cost of their exploitation.

Their adoption of these tools do not preclude them from remaining the target of exploitation, racism, and exclusion. According to Lorde's estimation, strategic Black participation in capitalism may not utterly "dismantle the master's house" in our lifetime, but there is evidence that it can and has already proven to make the house more equitable and just. The conscious use of capitalism's tools can create new conditions of possibility to both "beat him [the master] at his own game" and "enable us to bring about genuine change."[3]

The spaces of Black Capitalism—like Wall Street, social trends like soft living and hustle culture, popular culture and television, Africa and the diaspora—gesture toward transformational possibility. The undercommons of Wall Street make a case for change on the individual at the collective and institutional levels. Participation in investment banks, hedge funds, private equity firms, and the like is one vehicle to achieving financial stability for oneself and one's community, and redistributing different forms of capital. Choosing to navigate this terrain has the potential to shift the trajectory of someone's life toward what Jay-Z calls financial freedom.

◆ ◆ ◆

One of the most conflicting opportunities for institutional change is Black Capitalist participation in corporate America's persistent moral reckoning. Corporate attention to its own racist and exclusionary practice has ebbed and flowed with the zeitgeist, gaining traction only when the bottom line is in jeopardy by the threat of reputational risk exposure. Correcting deeply embedded structural inequality usually requires accepting uncompensated labor time and assuming responsibility as one of the few, if not the only, Black voices burdened with corporate transformation.

Despite the warning signs, many find meaningful ways to redesign the "master's house": volunteering their time to recruit and retain Black talent; serving on a thought leadership committee; building internal, grassroots programs to increase an organization's cultural competency; empowering external communities by teaching financial literacy; or the technical work of allocating corporate investment (not just charitable) dollars to support communities affected by systemic inequality. The net outcome of these efforts advances the goal of change more than the absence of them, and as imperfect as the institutions that make up Wall Street or corporate America are, their continued presence is likely. Cautiously working within the undercommons of these spaces to create sustainable resource channels can catalyze more iterative and expansive forms of Black thriving. The question we all must answer is whether the *possibility* of Black thriving in abundance is cause enough to try.

But remember, expressions of Black Capitalism are as diverse as Black people themselves. There's no one way to engage in capitalism with the intent to produce collective social good. And there's no one way to solve the problems of capitalism we experience today. But a productive starting point is reckoning with the tension inherent in using the master's tools to serve a new and equitable purpose for us all. My own experience as a business owner has taught me sobering truths about power and control in the employer-employee dynamic and their ability to rupture a community. I'll never forget Reggie, one of my former Black male employees, and his last words to me.

After a successful run at our brick-and-mortar location, I made the decision to close the shop to move Kelewele into the e-commerce and wholesale business. It was a smart move that would eliminate the lion's share of overhead costs and give me time to focus on scaling the business rather than getting caught in the weeds of restaurant operations. I was looking forward to the pivot.

But I was worried about my staff, whom I would effectively be laying off on our closing day, at least until I built the infrastructure for the new business model. I wanted to ensure that they were adequately supported, and so we spent the weeks leading up to our last day together brainstorming their professional interests and strategizing how to secure their next job.

By closing day, I was relieved to know that each member of my team had a plan for next steps that they were excited about. We spent most of that day cleaning and laughing about memorable customer service stories. I turned off the lights for the last time at seven p.m. As we collected our things, Reggie took off his stained yellow apron and said with great satisfaction, "I don't have to be a slave to Massa Rachel no more!" I stood frozen in disbelief. My Black female manager who overheard Reggie gasped in shock at his audacity. I didn't say anything, but I couldn't stop thinking about Reggie's comment in the weeks that followed.

I knew it was best to take the comment in stride. Reggie had told me and others on multiple occasions how much he enjoyed working at Kelewele, but even still, the harmless remark hurt. My efforts to create a flat organizational structure and offer professional development opportunities to balance the monotony of restaurant operations were reduced to an exploitative relationship between a "massa" and her laborers. I liked to think that I was enacting social good by employing young people within my community and nurturing their personal and professional development, but the experience forced me to confront the tension of being a well-intentioned capitalist.

I felt that my thankless efforts to create value for all of us, not just myself, were taken for granted, and with that came a feeling of defeat. I wasn't looking for praise, but the lack of acknowledgment that things were different at Kelewele made me wonder, "What's the point?"

"Girl, don't sweat it. He'll learn soon enough just how good he had it!" laughed one of my girlfriends after listening to me vent. As my mind ran a playback of some of my own loathsome work experiences, I could only hope her premonition was wrong. Reggie would leave Kelewele to take courses in artificial intelligence to break into the tech industry, but his lighthearted joke exposed how some young Black people today are talking about their relationship to capitalism, haphazardly or not. I've heard millennials, Generation Xers, and baby boomers describe their workplace as a metaphorical plantation to draw a loose comparison to what it can feel like to be a laborer in a modern-day exploitative economy. But never had I heard a twenty-year-old—the furthest removed from chattel slavery, Jim Crow, and the civil rights movement—describe their experience this way. The history of American slavery has an intergenerational grip on our discourse of capitalism and our place within it.

As a business owner, my responsibility to drive business profitability and my bottom line doesn't change. But starting honest conversation about the living history of American capitalism we feel and carry with us, and what can collectively be done about it can make a difference in how we all experience capitalism. And it's my responsibility to do so. Getting real about our anxieties, fears, and dreams about having money, not having enough of it, being dominated and controlled, and everything in between is the first step in challenging the scarcity mindset that shapes the version of capitalism that many Black people know today. There's a tax on being a capitalist when you're Black.

◆ ◆ ◆

The body of Black entrepreneurs, financiers, gig workers, hustlers, and soft and luxury lifers is growing. We all have a slice of capitalism's pie. And so we all have a part to play. But, as I have argued here and will continue to argue, the practice of Black Capitalism—an economic process whereby actors (individual and collective) proactively reposition themselves within capitalism to achieve social good—is a blueprint for a new kind of capitalism. And coupled with alternative forms of resistance, that new capitalism can correct the harms of American capitalism and produce multiple modes of Black thriving in service of Black liberation.

In a viral tweet, the Black American rapper Robert "Meek Mill" Williams wrote, "We in the easiest time to become a millionaire . . . don't be a weirdo let's go!!!"[4] The comment is cheeky and humorous at first pass but inspires further reflection. What does it mean to be a "weirdo" in this case? Arguably, it means holding allegiance to a historical narrative that posits a productive relationship between Black people and wealth as untenable.

This thinking is at the crux of critiques lobbed against Black Capitalists in their journey to realize capital accumulation to produce social good. My challenge to this kind of thinking is not a dismissal of the systemic inequalities that make stories of Black economic thriving exceptional and often elitist, but is instead a call to action.

When we fully understand the difference race can make in one's participation in capitalism and collectively choose to engage in capitalism with a shared goal, stories of Black thriving can become the norm instead of being exceptional. The possibility of more instances of Black thriving makes the practice of Black Capitalism compelling and worth our collective attention as we strive to close the racial wealth gap.

Resistance to the structures that oppress people and reproduce inequality is complicated, contradictory, and varied in its expression. Appreciating just how diverse acts of resistance can be gets us one step closer to elevating our collective consciousness about how Black people can relate to capital and the social good that can be produced as a by-product of that relationship.

When we pay attention to the multiple forms of thriving Black Capitalism can produce, we expand our thinking about the requirements for meaningful social change, theories of racial capitalism, and Black liberation. The multiple spaces in which we find Black Capitalism at work is a reminder that despite the cost placed on Blackness, it can make a productive difference in how we wield the tools of capitalism to create new conditions of economic possibility that bend toward a more just and equitable world for all of us. Though this work is tremendously hard and demands the best version of ourselves in how we think and relate to one another, it is both necessary and the way forward to create new conditions of thriving for all of us.

Korle Gonno

I spent most of high school suppressing my African identity and most of college and the start of my professional career working so hard, I had little time to sit and ponder the existential question "Who am I and what inspires me?" But an exchange with a man I was dating at the time brought my worries—that were bubbling up under the surface—to a head and prompted my sojourn back home to Africa.

Grayson was handsome. A looming six feet with caramel locs and skin that looked like butterscotch in the peak of summertime. A Brooklyn–born Trinidadian, he was an artist who dabbled in interior design, painting, sculpture, spoken word poetry, and more. He was nine years older than me and protested formal work as the pitfall of capitalism meant to keep Black people down. Most days he grumbled about "going to the plantation" during our morning subway rides into Manhattan. The militant aspects of his personality found home in the teachings of the Black Panther Party, which he studied with a community of other diligent Black students. We were an unlikely pair, but I was attracted to his creative energy, and he valued my ambition.

He supported me as I wrestled with imposter syndrome while trying to find my footing at Goldman Sachs even as more and more of my contributions to our conversations soon became stories about my work projects, the people I was meeting at the firm, or the latest work drama I was circumventing. He always appeared to be listening, but one day in the middle of a Key Foods in downtown Brooklyn he stopped to look at me and said, "I don't want to lose you."

Those words were an intervention. I was allowing my job to

consume my life, which was pushing people out in the process. For the first time, I was confronted with the fact that I had never made the time to do more than compartmentalize my nagging feelings about who I really was. Looking back at his freckled face, which was painted in concern, I thought to myself, "I don't want to lose me either."

My grandmother's home in Korle Gonno, by Ghana's seaside, was the first and only place I thought to go to ground myself. My mom and uncles told me stories I could no longer remember about me as a toddler living in the multistory white home adorned with exotic plants and wildflowers while my mom was in the United States hustling to save enough money so that Dash and I could live with her in a decent home. It's where I forced my grandma to chase me up and down the grand tan-and-salmon terrazzo staircase as I ran away with delight. It's also where I acquired the scar that sits above my right eyebrow—a consequence of running too fast on the marble flooring and splitting my forehead open, which required stitches from the family doctor.

In that house my grandma would sit for hours in the outdoor vestibule making the most delicious light soup and fufu on a charcoal stove because she feared having gas-powered equipment in the house. By the time my mom returned to Korle Gonno to take me back to the United States, I cried incessantly, begging for my mom, not knowing the woman I yearned for was actually my grandma.

I'd visited in the years prior, but this time was different. I went alone as a young adult curious to make meaning of my Ghanaian identity on my own terms. In America I felt too African, and in Africa I felt too American. But in my grandmother's house, I was just right. As my grandma's legs had grown weak in her old age, she now preferred to spend most of her time sitting in one of the family's branded chairs on the indoor verandah that overlooked the nearby shantytown. The chairs, in beige, rusty orange, and mocha, were embossed with the Adinkra symbol Gye Nyame wrapped around the name of my family's hospitality business.[5] Nonetheless, when I arrived for my two-week stay, my grandmother greeted me with a comforting smile and her usual two-part question, "Hello, Naa-Du, have you eaten and are you hungry?"

Korle Gonno had changed over the decades—it was once a quiet beach town sprinkled with beautiful homes built by prosperous community members—and it was now an overpopulated neighborhood housing many Ghanaian migrants who traveled to the capital in search of work. My grandmother watched both the changes and the things that stayed the same, like the tall mango and coconut trees that sprouted like weeds, even in a concrete landscape.

I'd pull a chair next to her so I could see what she saw and listen to her stories. She told me about selling textiles and home goods before she became a wife and mother to ten children. And how she ran the family's multiple businesses after the passing of my grandfather. She had a no-nonsense approach and always kept meticulous accounting and oversight of all her operations. In the local business community, people knew better than to cheat her.

Grandma was also a landlord. Often as we sat together her tenants would visit with their rent payments in hand. We'd all make small talk as she put on her glasses to review the handwritten ledger that kept records of hundreds of tenant payments. Watching my five-foot-tall grandma draped in one of her vibrant kaftans while seated in her veranda chair running her real estate business was something I'd never appreciated until then. The Ghanaian real estate business is known to be ruthless, risky, and run largely by men. But Grandma held her own, which demanded the respect and recognition of others, a hard thing for a woman to achieve in a male-dominated business. I beamed with pride at the sight of her and the knowledge that I was the grandchild of such an influential woman. Her presence inspired a new standard in me for the kind of impact I should aspire to have. I wanted to be just like her.

After tenants would bring their payments in bundles of cash, Grandma would also gift whoever was in the house at the time—uncles, aunts, cousins, and even family friends—with a portion of the net profits. The first time I witnessed her do this, I returned her smile with a puzzled look as she handed me my portion. My uncle Ebo, my grandmother's youngest child, piped up to clarify. "She does this all the time," he said. "She's taught us that you have to give in order to receive in life." Through her actions, Grandma modeled to me, and everyone else, what it means to be a Black Capitalist.

Her giving didn't stop there. She invested in enough land to create entire neighborhoods so that my aunts and uncles could build communities of their own. Grandma gifted her children with properties next to each other so that her family would always have a reason to stay connected while living comfortably. She never called her actions "generational wealth building," but rather "community building." For her, it was implied that when we operate with a community mindset, everyone benefits. She was the matriarch of the family: powerful, not to be messed with, beloved, and respected.

The more I learned about Grandma, the more curious I became about my grandpa too. He died of a heart attack when my mom was nineteen and still living in Korle Gonno with her brothers and sisters. I never knew him, but his spirit felt alive in the home he once shared with my grandmother. I asked Uncle Ebo many questions about Grandpa: "What was he like? Was he like Grandma? How did he build the family business?"

"Here, start with this," he said, and handed me a tattered magazine turned to a full-page feature of my grandpa.

A pioneer hotelier, in 1936 he established one of the first hotels in Ghana, then called the Gold Coast. The facility became a "magnet which pulled in guests from all over Ghana and Africa"— as well as the United States, the United Kingdom, Switzerland, Germany, and Scandinavia—who needed reliable accommodation in Accra.[6] As my grandfather was a "workaholic in every sense," his establishment offered restaurant and catering services, a cocktail bar, a craft shop, and a minimart for the convenience of his guests and the general public.[7] For business executives who came to Accra from different parts of the world, the only place they could go for adequate lodging was my grandfather's hotel. And as a result, the hotel became a popular venue for weddings and conferences.

The article talked about how my grandfather, who was from the Ga tribe in Jamestown, studied in Accra and started his adult life as a professional draftsman in 1929. He launched his venture in the hospitality industry after studying the business terrain in the country's city and identifying an unmet need. Not only was he a visionary, but he was also an educationist. He founded a school in the Gold Coast and served as the principal, training many young women and men who became prominent citizens. He also established a trade and technical institute to teach young people the craft of draftsmanship. People also knew him for his sayings, like "No sweat, no sweet," "Hard work is the great secret of success," and "No pain, no gain." He died in 1985 "as one of the hard-working personalities who helped to establish the hotel business" in Ghana.[8]

I read the article over and over, memorizing the words, and stared at the black-and-white headshot of my grandfather. He was tall, broad-shouldered, and dressed to the nines with a quizzical stare. His full head of white hair looked like a crown of bunched-up cotton balls, a striking contrast to the richness of his melanated skin, which shone. Looking at him, I realized just how much I missed his life and him, though I never knew him. Reading his vision and witnessing the reality of it reminded me of dreams I'd buried only to dig up if I were brave enough. "No sweat, no sweet," I imagined him saying as I sat there with his picture and life story resting in the palm of my hand.

My trip home was a call to action. It taught me from whom I had come, the legacy of my grandparents that was built through hard work and determination, and my responsibility to preserve and expand their vision of community building in a way that felt authentic to me. Seeing my grandmother and learning about my grandfather made me feel accountable for the well-being of my family today, but even more so for future family members I may never meet. Witnessing my grandparents' commitment to leaving behind an inheritance of love for community, ethical principles, and financial security for their children's children, many of whom my grandfather never met, inspired a passion in me to do the same. It means that their sacrifice was not made in vain, and that the possibility of Black thriving within my family line does not end with me.

I also left Korle Gonno with a new perspective on my employment. Those within my family who knew what Goldman Sachs was were proud of me for being part of such an elite and competitive space. My being there meant that they were there too, which was a win for all of us. Grandma had no idea what the firm was and didn't care so long as I was well fed and taking good care of myself in the Big Apple. I appreciated my family's approval, but I knew then I had it in me to be more than a Wall Street professional for the rest of my career. My uncles would often jokingly say, "We're counting on you to carry the name further. Make it *big* in America," but this time, I took it seriously.

The trip forced me to step outside of the monotonous grind of working and start asking harder questions. What would it take to see us stop suffering so much—not just throughout the diaspora, but in Africa too? There had to be more for us than our presumed birthright to scarcity and lack. How could I help make even the smallest difference to prove it? I wanted not only to search for answers but also to uncover what the meaning of those answers could teach us about how to interact with the political economy feeling empowered and oriented toward communal care and longevity.

The principles my grandmother lived by as an entrepreneur and community builder—seek to do well financially and always do right by others—was the starting point to question and explore how thriving can become commonplace in the Black experience. Fast-forward, I'd go on to learn about how Black people were creating community in the undercommons of Wall Street, but there was an even bigger story to tell. What can it look like to thrive in capitalism for those who leave the undercommons of Wall Street but stay in the financial industry as entrepreneurs operating on the African continent?

PART 2

The Pan-African Dream

CHAPTER 8

The Best Is Yet to Come

I returned to Ghana in the winter of 2018 as an anthropologist in search of answers to my questions. The following year would be pivotal for the country. Formally dubbed as the "Year of Return" by Ghanaian president Nana Akufo-Addo, 2019 served as a twelve-month commemoration of the contributions and sacrifices made by enslaved Africans first brought to English colonies in Virginia four hundred years ago. There was also an invitation to Africans living across the diaspora to return home and invest in the African continent, and especially Ghana.

The Ministry of Tourism partnered with local and international vendors to curate a year's worth of events, including the Back2Africa Festival, the Marcus Garvey Award Ball and Banquet, the Jamestown-to-Jamestown African American Summit, the Chale Wote Festival, an investment forum, and the Afro-Future Festival. The Year of Return made it cool to be Ghanaian, which felt foreign given my upbringing. My patriotism made me happy with the visibility these events gave this small West

African country. But still, I wondered, "Who would benefit from all this?"

Leading up to my arrival in Accra, I was curious and anxious to know how preparations for the upcoming year were playing out on the ground. On WhatsApp phone calls with friends and family, it seemed that locals knew little of what the Year of Return even was and had a healthy skepticism about who would profit most from it. I was keen to learn firsthand of any differences between how the Year of Return was marketed globally and who it affected locally.

I had traveled to Ghana several times previously, and the arrival gate always had a quietness about it, as if all the travelers had made this journey before. But upon arriving at Kotoka International Airport and being met with Ghana's dry summer heat, I could sense a difference in the atmosphere this time.

A buzz filled the airport as Black diasporans crowded the "Foreigners" section of the customs checkpoint and I eavesdropped on conversations about where some of these new visitors would dine, stay, and tour while in Ghana. I made my way through customs and baggage check, conversing in my broken Ga whenever airport staff and security would check my passport, read my Ghanaian name—Naa-Du Laryea—and then immediately perked up with excitement about my return home. The guards at the customs gate were always fascinated by my Ghanaian heritage because it took them by surprise. They read me as an American, and so every time I offered up my Ghanaian passport to be stamped, they had questions. And they also had pride that I'd come home because at some point they'd come to believe that a young Ghanaian born in America would not return.

Hundreds of people crowded the outdoor arrival area, and

with my two bulging suitcases, carry-on duffel, and backpack on my shoulders, I scanned the crowd looking for my uncles as I turned down taxi drivers waiting for their next customer. "Rachel," I heard someone yell out but struggled to place the sound. Finally, I made eye contact with my uncle Isaac, a six-foot-tall businessman who I could expect to be dressed in his standard thick-sole black shoes, navy-blue slacks, and a tucked-in collared linen shirt. My uncle Ebo followed close behind in his usual street wear—a graphic tee, baggy jeans, and skater shoes.

We loaded my luggage into Uncle Isaac's black Ford truck and made our way out of the airport parking lot. The influx of travelers exacerbated the already poor traffic conditions in the country's capital and the normally twenty-five-minute car ride from the airport to Korle Gonno took an hour and a half. At times, Uncle Isaac even turned off the engine, finding it senseless to waste fuel as we sat in traffic. Car horns blasted in the background. Ghanaian gospel music boomed from street-corner speakers, and mobile street vendors weaved through the roads selling everything from tires and toiletries to plantain chips and tiger nuts.

We chatted about Ghanaian political corruption, my studies at Yale, and life in the United States. "It's not as amazing as they make it seem," I found myself repeating to my uncles. They had traveled through parts of Europe but never the United States, and they were convinced it was more advanced and sophisticated than our motherland. On every visit home we spoke about the American Dream, and despite my best efforts to add a healthy dose of realism to my family's perception of the "land of the free," they always countered with the adage "In America, hard work pays off."

From their vantage point as Ghanaian citizens living in the

country, avenues for achieving prosperity were few for those at the bottom of the socioeconomic ladder. And the truth was that their sister, my mother, left Ghana in her mid-twenties in search of greater opportunities for herself and children and found it—with a lot of work—in the form of homeownership, access to scholarships for her children to attend excellent schools, and lucrative careers as well as fully funded doctorate degrees. As far as my uncles could tell, I was living proof that the American Dream is not just a dream, but a reality.

But this sojourn home also felt different because my grandmother wasn't there. Sadness in the form of a deep, slow breath left my lungs when we finally arrived at her house and I saw my grandmother's empty chair for the first time. Somehow, I thought it wouldn't be empty. As if her death were something I'd made up. I was writing midterm exams when she passed away, and I used that as an excuse to avoid the pain of seeing her body, now lifeless, one more time.

So while others celebrated, I mourned the loss I'd returned to. The most I could do was pull up a chair next to hers and look out the window, watching the leaves of the coconut and mango trees sway in the wind, taking in all that had changed and all that had stayed the same.

I took comfort in visits from my grandmother's old friends (even though I didn't remember most of them), who streamed in and out of the house, bringing with them nostalgic stories of the past and cooking food slowly the way she used to. With the help of Ayeley, our family housekeeper, we made all my favorite meals: fufu with groundnut soup, a bean stew called red red, kontomire stew made from cocoyam leaves with boiled yam, a black-eyed pea and rice dish called waakye, and even kelewele.

Uncle Ebo kept me company since he had moved into my

grandmother's house. He also rented out a section of the house, a responsibility he inherited when he and his brothers and sisters divided the work of maintaining my grandmother's real estate, hospitality, and agriculture businesses. I stayed in the guest room connected to my grandmother's, where her closets, filled with yards of her gorgeous wax prints and custom jewelry, remained untouched. My closeness to her things made me feel just a bit closer to her.

◆ ◆ ◆

For the duration of my stay, I had arranged to shadow two entrepreneurs: Wemimo Abbey and Sangu Delle. I thought of them as Black Capitalists because of how they were innovating the financial services industry through their community-centered thinking. Wemimo was the cofounder and co–chief executive officer of Esusu Financial Incorporated, a U.S.-based fintech company that automates credit building by reporting monthly rent payments to credit bureaus. What struck me about Wemimo's work was that Esusu was at the vanguard of building a tool that had the potential to unlock access to better credit health or a new credit history for millions of people. Those best positioned to benefit from Esusu's technology were the economically disenfranchised. And due to the racial wealth gap in this country, the people in question were disproportionately people of color. Why is this important? Because as Jay-Z raps in "The Story of O.J." on the *4:44* album, good credit is the key to financial freedom in America.

I had met Wemimo during our first day of training as Goldman Sachs interns in the spring of 2015. We were seated next to each other for an afternoon session on the fundamentals of investment banking as the instructor breezed through dozens of PowerPoint slides. I was struggling to keep my anxiety at bay as I took long, deep breaths to calm the feeling of panic that was creeping up inside my chest. Meanwhile, Wemimo was enjoying himself—asking rhetorical questions just loud enough for me to hear, which I took as an invitation for conversation. He was dressed sharply in a tailored navy-blue suit with a checked sky-blue tie placed neatly between the points of his crisp white collar. His almond-brown eyes were energetic, and his playful smile had a gap between his two front teeth that reminded me of my mom's. If the saying "Say it with your chest" were a person, it would be Wemimo. It was refreshing to see and hear a confident Black man in a room of more than one hundred interns wherein I could count the number of Black people on two hands. His insight and presence felt equally precious to me.

I would complete my internship in the firm's Corporate Services and Real Estate Division, and he in Risk Management. We didn't see much of each other that summer and lost touch. But almost a year later, while wrapping up my final semester of undergrad at NYU, I ran into Wemimo in the West Village, a few blocks away from Washington Square Park in Manhattan. Turns out he was completing his master's degree at NYU's Wagner School of Public Service. We promised to stay in touch and did so here and there at first, then grew a deeper friendship in 2018 when I launched my small business and he was there to lend a helping hand.

As I watched Wemimo grow his fintech startup over the same year I developed my research study on Black Capitalism, I knew his story and the kinds of questions it inspires would be invaluable to my work. I was delighted when he agreed to take part in my study. Most of our conversations took place over

Zoom or the phone, but by the end of the summer, we discovered that we'd both be ending the year in Ghana—a place he endearingly calls his "second home." Wemimo first traveled to Ghana in 2012 as a college student and the founder of a nonprofit that built wells throughout West Africa.

I met him at his shared apartment in East Legon, which was owned by a woman Wemimo called his Ghanaian auntie. When traveling through Accra I prefer to take trotros, privately owned minibuses that, while fast and affordable, have a reputation for being unsafe. In the vehicles, it's not unusual to find people crowded on top of one another or for a car seat to be worn, broken, or even missing. But I like trotros because of their local feel and the opportunity to listen in on the conversations between people sitting so close to one another. "Chale, you're putting your life in your hands, ooo," my friends often tease, but I never listen.

But securing a trotro from Korle Gonno to East Legon and back in the late evening would prove challenging, so I tried my luck using Uber for the first time in Accra. I was pleasantly surprised by the accuracy of my Uber driver's global positioning system, as many roads in the Korle Gonno area lack signs or are unnamed. We sped down the George Walker Bush Highway (a major highway financed by the American Millennium Challenge Account during the Bush administration), arriving at my destination in record time. It was a rare, quiet Wednesday evening with few drivers on the road.

I took notice of the compound and surrounding neighborhood as the security guard, dressed in a pressed white collared uniform, greeted me warmly. Wealth was etched into the grand and brightly painted concrete homes, well-maintained greenery, and landscaping. Luxury cars filled the driveway as I walked up the glass staircase to the second floor of the building. From there I caught a bird's-eye view of the town adorned with Christmas trees and lights.

Wemimo welcomed me into a large apartment decorated with plush furniture and modern amenities. Shortly after I arrived, an attendant rang the doorbell carrying a heaping plate of jollof rice, grilled chicken, sauteed vegetables, and a tall glass of pineapple juice for Wemimo. After I insisted multiple times that I did not want any refreshments (which likely meant a large meal rather than a snack, given Ghanaian hospitality), the attendant left us to chat.

A self-identified "global citizen," Wemimo was born into an upper-middle-class family in Lagos, Nigeria, in 1992. "I was one of those kids taken to school in a Mercedes in the early 1990s," he said. But all of that changed when his father died without a will, leaving the two-year-old Wemimo and his mother unable to access his wealth. He and his mother were forced to move to a remote part of the city into an uncompleted house his mother had started building in secret while his father was still alive. The project was conducted in secrecy because at that time the wife of a wealthy man was not expected to be industrious outside of the home. Doing so was frowned upon because it broke gender norms among the well-to-do and challenged the convention (perhaps based on the male ego) that a man is the only one who can provide for the family. Her proper place was in the home, not a construction site. But his mom thought otherwise, since her ambitions surpassed the household. So Wemimo and his mother moved into the cement building without a functioning toilet in the slums of Lagos.

"Mom is a fighter and arguably one of the most respected women I know," Wemimo told me. "She provided for me the best way she could. With hard work and perseverance, we built the house while living in it. There were nights we got rained on. Most nights mosquitoes and stray cats were our closest neighbors. That's all I knew. Just a fighting spirit which my mother provided and the faith that the best was yet to come."

Wemimo's mother also never wavered in her belief that, as he put it, "education was the most paramount investment any child could have." And she ensured that Wemimo had access to what he describes as "one of the finest educations a young man could ask for" at Federal Government College in Lagos.

Wemimo had a stubborn confidence that he could be whatever he set his mind to. And attending school with the children of top government officials produced in him the reverse effect of imposter syndrome. "People had the same head, two eyes, one mouth and baseline intellectual capability," he said. "I wouldn't let my economic deficit take over. I positioned my difference as a strength and a challenge to push forward." Even still, he added, "money was everything" as he saw the "injustice in full force of what it means to not have capital."

Wemimo's mother tried her best to shelter him from the reality of their financial situation, going as far as lying to him that his father was still alive to shield him from the magnitude of her responsibilities. He believed that his father was away on business in the United States until around the age of ten, when he finally overheard during a family meeting that his father was dead. Despite his mother's desire to protect him from the truth for years, Wemimo knew that his mother's paychecks never quite added up to enough.

From an early age, he started selling American candy like Kit Kats—sent from his older sister in Texas—to wealthy classmates. In the 1980s, before Wemimo was born, his mother traveled to the United States, where she gave birth to his sister so that she could have the privilege of American citizenship. They came back to Nigeria afterward, but his sister ultimately returned to the United States for college and kept her little brother in mind by sending him treats when she could. But survival mentality kicked in, and Wemimo knew that if he ate all the bags of candy his sister sent, he wouldn't have anything to show for it later.

In middle and high school, he developed a credible reputation for supplying legitimate American chocolate, so when he did run out of stock, he'd source local chocolate and sell it at a 100 percent markup without concern because by then he'd built a brand and no one could write him off. From chocolates he graduated to Game Boys. His most lucrative commodity was the Pokemon Crystal, which sold at "very good margins," he recalled. He then started selling PlayStation II games and consoles while managing the growing local demand and the timing of his sister's international shipments. The capital he accumulated helped pay for the schoolbooks and SAT prep books that he used to study fastidiously and prime himself for an opportunity to attend college in the United States. He describes America as "the greatest country in the world" because it's in America that someone can give you millions of dollars to build a business thanks to little more than a ten-page pitch deck, passion, and persistence. For Wemimo, in America, the quality of an idea means something.

"Why did you opt to study at the University of Minnesota rather than the prestigious University of Lagos, where you were admitted to after high school?" I asked.

He said, "I grew up *in* and *with* nothing. I fundamentally understood as a kid that I have be audacious and know that I have nothing to fall back on. I had to chart a path forward and live the life I believe I was destined for. My fundamental purpose is to explore the road less traveled. The best I could do with nothing to fall back on was to fall forward. I always take the biggest risk because even if I don't get it, it costs me nothing." He was also inspired by the hope and promise of President Barack Obama's 2008 election and wanted to be part of American history in the making.

Wemimo migrated to the United States during a Minnesota winter "with a three-piece suit, excited for the good life." The culture shock was immediate. In addition to not understanding "why people choose to live in freezers," he struggled to adjust to "America's sugar-coating culture," having been raised to be direct. For the first time, he also reckoned with what it meant for him to be a Black man in America. Despite his continued financial challenges, and sobering experiences with racism and law enforcement, Wemimo's upbringing taught him how to be "strong against all odds." Wemimo learned at an early age that "if one can control a product and its supply and demand chain, one can dictate their economic situation," so he decided to study business. His entrepreneurial spirit became a by-product of his former need to participate in survival entrepreneurship.

While in college, he launched his first business, Clean Water for Everyone (CWE), a student-led nonprofit focused on providing affordable water to developing countries. He could sense my next question at this point in the conversation because he continued by declaring, "Every company I've started has a personal story." The creation of CWE was in response to Wemimo having nearly lost his life to typhoid while in high school in Nigeria. Upon his college graduation, Wemimo disbanded CWE and transitioned ownership of its projects to the local communities and municipalities in the countries it serviced with intent to give "the power to the people to move the frontiers of their lives forward." Some of those projects continue to this day.

While his academic interests were rooted in the principles of humanitarianism (he took courses in public policy and development finance at UC Berkeley and NYU), the theory and practice of finance underpinned his studies, which turned his attention to Wall Street. His graduate school peers called Wemimo a sellout for accepting an offer at Goldman Sachs while they went on to work at the United Nations and the World Health Organization.

At the firm, Wemimo forged relationships within the undercommons, but his daily work life left much to be desired. He faced alienation for questioning senior leaders on his team who championed what he considered to be a "problematic status quo." He could not bring his "best self to work" without being seen as threatening to those around him, which was one of the reasons for his short career at the firm.

Wemimo's experience was proof that despite corporate claims embracing diversity, the practice of such was lacking. The other driver of Wemimo's short stint at the investment bank was his vision for his professional career. "I never thought I'd be a partner at Goldman," he said. "I'm an entrepreneur. People can sniff that in me. I think like a business owner. My perspective on it was: Learn as much as I can at the fastest pace possible and move on with life." After leaving Goldman Sachs, Wemimo worked in mergers and acquisitions at PricewaterhouseCoopers (PWC), where he stayed for almost three years executing deals worth close to $50 billion combined. He was excited by the work, well positioned to be promoted rapidly, and viewed as a superstar by his colleagues. But he knew staying at PWC for the long term would be settling. So instead, he leveraged the professional experiences and expertise he'd gained as a bridge to entrepreneurship, which gave rise to his company, Esusu.

The first iteration of Esusu took shape toward the latter half of Wemimo's career at PWC, where he forged a business partnership with Samir Goel, a friend he met years before at an event organized by the Clinton Foundation. The cofounders were aligned on their desire to make a lasting impact on the world rooted in their lived experiences. Working a full-time job while building Esusu's foundation was intense but offered rare opportunities, such as an invitation to pitch Esusu on the NASDAQ floor. Their presentation garnered curiosity by industry experts and gave Wemimo the last bit of validation he needed to leave PWC: "As a Black man, I don't have the privilege of the Mark Zuckerbergs of the world who can pitch an idea and expect immediate investors. I needed to know my stuff and Goldman and PWC gave me the pedigree and skill set to build a reputable business based on competency."

The catalyst behind Esusu is both personal and equitable. "I was raised by a single mother who had to make miracles out of nothing," Wemimo told me. "She was on salary barely surviving paycheck to paycheck and still had to pay for my education." Wemimo's mother pooled money with family and friends, which is a lending process called *susu*. It's one of the oldest forms of banking, resource control, and a means to build people's financial identity. That traditional money-lending practice led to the creation of Esusu. The idea was simple: "We aspired to digitize the traditional practice and give forty-seven million immigrants around the world the opportunity to do it. At the core of whatever we do as a race, having access to credit and opportunities from a financial standpoint is what paves the way to access. I saw it as a major gap and asked myself how I could contribute and help others based on my skill set."

Esusu's origin story reveals the venture's mission-driven approach to business, but I was curious how the mission could produce a transformation in financial practice. "So what sets you apart from any other fintech founder?" I asked.

"I'm a different kind of finance guy. I'm a social entrepreneur. I'm deeply invested in amassing wealth and redistributing the wealth to level the playing field for others," he said. He went on to share his lack of interest in the status quo and the "draconian way the winner takes all, and steps on the little one as they ascend to the top with all of their wealth." He paused as his eyes met mine. "I'm not like that. I don't associate with that. I'm the person that wants to get as much wealth as possible, deploy it in society, and make it catalytic. Ensure other people who look like me, or have a similar background as me, or worse, have a fighting chance."

Although Esusu is a digital business, physical proximity to those Wemimo aims to empower is critical to the company's vision. Wemimo and his cofounder were intentional about situating Esusu's headquarters in Harlem to channel the Silicon Harlem movement, and Harlem's legacy as a birthplace for Black renaissance.[1] Esusu also has its sights on the African continent. Wemimo has built a social network that taps into the higher echelons of government in Ghana, Uganda, and Kenya, and he believes the global nature of the business will grow quickly once launched. "We are audacious in our want to center Africa in our vision to build a platform that will create global credit scores for people," he explained. "The African landscape plays a quintessential role in our growth moving forward, and the continent has a lot of opportunities to leverage the tech we built."

Today, global credit scores don't exist. And Esusu is building on a well-established practice widespread throughout the continent. In the African market, its value proposition is offering consumers credit identity, creating accessibility to that formalized identity, cash flow management, and the ability to advise national governments on tax decisions. "We want to reimagine the impossible and the road less traveled," Wemimo said. "The inspiration behind that is that I've traveled to different places, but my credit identity didn't travel with me. When my mother and I moved to the United States, we didn't have cash and my mom had to sell her wedding ring so that we could have cash. It shouldn't be that way."

When I pressed Wemimo to talk about the implications of transferring Western business principles into an African context, he doubled down on his claims but with a hint of defensiveness: "I have the right to say it because I've lived here. The African continent is lagging behind in development, rule of law, regulatory policies among other things. It is not as sharp as what we have in the Western world." The opportunity he sees is pairing the creative ideas coming out of the continent, like the creation of mobile money (the ability to send and receive money via a mobile device), with "old, tried, and true pedigree infrastructure that's present in the West." He could sense I was hanging on to each word as he continued: "It's about how we can take what works in the West—consumer financial protection, regulatory frameworks, management reporting, and tax policy, which, yes, isn't perfect—and what works in the East—technological innovation—and bring that together and use it to build something new and fresh. The aim is to try and champion new ideas while capturing what is already working in different places. It's not about copying and pasting—that's not the right approach."

The outcomes of Wemimo's strategy in an African context have yet to be fully realized, as the work to establish working partnerships with African countries remains underway. But this kind of thinking has global reach and targets those who have been intentionally and historically ignored in the creation of credit and generational wealth building.

The Afrobeats Wemimo's roommate was playing in the living room behind the home office we occupied was growing louder, and a small party was forming. I could hear more voices and laughter penetrating through the wall. At that moment I recalled Wemimo's earlier invitation for me to join him and others at Twist Club that evening and realized his apartment was the location for the pre-game.

I quickly worked my way through questions I wanted to ask in person since I did not know when we would have time like this again. We talked about his affinity for the term *Black Capitalist* and his willing participation in capitalism because "we haven't yet found another economic system that works, albeit imperfectly." Instantly reading the curiosity on my face, he laughed and promised to reserve time for a follow-up discussion on his theory and practice of capitalism.

When I asked him if there was anything else he wanted to share, he paused, looked down at his now empty plate, and then looked back at me to say: "As a Black entrepreneur, you have to work ten times as hard, know your shit before you walk into a room, and you *might* be given a fighting chance. Genius is in abundance, but opportunities are few."

I lingered awhile and met Wemimo's roommate and friends, all of whom were the children of diplomats who had lived in Ghana and traveled the world. Wemimo moved through the room with ease, laughing, drinking, and striking up conversations. Although tempted to stay, I made my exit. Wemimo insisted on walking me out and staying with me as I waited for my Uber ride outside the lit building gates. After watching my Uber driver on the app drive around, clearly lost, I caught sight of him at the end of the block and frantically waved him down before he canceled the ride out of desperation. As my second driver pulled up in a bright yellow Hyundai Getz, Wemimo and I shared a parting hug, after which he smiled at me and said, "The best is yet to come."

On the ride home, I thought through Wemimo's desire to be an entrepreneur and determine his socioeconomic status. Wemimo's experience with poverty inspired, out of necessity, an affinity for entrepreneurship, a medium he hoped could create economic security for himself and others. It struck me that Wemimo never made mention of ever wanting to be wealthy for personal indulgence. Instead, he spoke of wanting financial control, which at its core is a type of freedom many Black people are never granted.

CHAPTER 9

Obroni

I spent the last days of 2018 closely following the Ministry of Tourism's campaign on the Year of Return. While the oral histories of my family lineage do not mention our involvement as sellers or captives of the Atlantic slave trade, it was important to me that I visit Cape Coast Castle on the first day of the new year to research and appreciate the experience of others.

The castle was one of the main slave dungeons along the coast owned by European traders at the height of the slave trade but is now a major tourist destination. It's known for its haunting design, which includes the black wooden "Door of Return" (previously "Door of No Return") dividing the slave dungeons and the Atlantic Ocean. The enslaved people who walked through that door would in fact never return. But the glimmer of hope that, despite this tragic reality, the progeny of those people might one day make the sojourn back home.

With my younger cousin Gogi, I took a charter bus from downtown Accra for the two-hour leg of the journey followed by a trotro that dropped us off along the hill where the castle stands. The sun was blazing, but the heat was dry and the ocean carried a relieving breeze. Along the outskirts of the castle's looming grounds, street sellers hustled for eye contact as they made attempts to sell mangoes, freshly picked coconuts, and bagged plantain chips. Their arms and hands were adorned with necklaces, bracelets, and rings, also for sale.

Upon entering the compound, we were greeted by a government employee who directed our attention to the left, where we would find the registration kiosk to purchase tour tickets. The sign that was affixed to the wall of the remodeled shipping container listed separate admission fees for foreigners and locals. I handed the attendant our Ghanaian identification and entry fees. Kojo, the male attendant, returned Gogi's ID to him with a tour pass and then turned to me and insisted I pay the foreigner fee. I exhaled in disappointment but wasn't surprised by the request. This happened to me often. Even though I was a Ghanaian citizen on paper, locals often labeled me as *obroni,* an Akan word meaning "foreigner" and colloquially used to describe a white person.

Without ever hearing me speak, many assumed I was a foreigner because of my lighter complexion, natural locs, and dress. In the past when I met others like Kojo who asserted their authority over me, I would argue my right to a Ghanaian identity. But over time I started to accept the consequence of being a hyphenated Ghanaian as I reckoned with the privileges afforded to me as an American citizen.

I handed over the remaining cedis, and Kojo gave me a tour pass, my Ghanaian passport still open to the biodata page. I whispered my name under my breath: Rachel Naa-Du Laryea. The dissonance of reading my Ga name on African soil while being stripped of my nationality by a fellow Ghanaian at a historic slave dungeon was both haunting and painful. Even as the waiting area began to fill with tourists, the feeling of isolation lingered in my chest. In the center of the crowd, I heard Kwame, our guide, begin the tour. A stocky five-foot-tall man with skin that had the look of freshly laid asphalt, Kwame had a soft voice, the kind that could deliver the most gruesome message to its recipient with gentleness.

He recited horrid facts of the living conditions of the enslaved people who were packed like sardines into the dungeons. At a point along the tour Kwame stopped us to say, "You should know that the ground you're standing on is not the actual ground of the dungeon but actually human waste that was hardened over time as these rooms were packed with people one on top of the other." People gasped in disgust. I and everyone else looked down at our feet. The silence among us spoke volumes. Aboveground, we visited the airy captors' quarters, the newly constructed museum, and the Door of Return. Kwame concluded his remarks after we reached the door, thanking everyone "for coming home."

The tour group disbanded. Some people hovered around Kwame eager to ask follow-up questions. Others walked down to the shore where fishing boats were docked and young boys were fooling around and swimming. Most moseyed around the castle's compound, taking photos and making small talk.

While my cousin Gogi took selfies, I sat along the castle walls by the cannons facing the sea. I gazed across the Atlantic Ocean with incredulity, and yet feelings of pride and hope began to stir up in me. For enslaved people to withstand such awful atrocities required a relentless resolve to not be broken. Their endurance made possible the return of their progeny, some of whom I saw before me.

Throughout the afternoon strangers chatted about how their Ancestry.com results traced their bloodlines to Ghana. A young woman in a Kente jumpsuit and bright yellow hat shared that this first trip was also a permanent move. "I couldn't stand to live in America anymore . . . the way they treat us there. . . ." She paused, furiously shaking her head. "It's not worth it. I had to leave. I've only been here for a few weeks and it already feels like more of a home than America ever was. I've been welcomed with open arms and it's been amazing."

Others shared in her joy as they talked about preparing to leave their respective corners of the African diaspora and repatriate home. As I exited the castle, I ran into Dwight, whom I'd met earlier in the day during our tour. He was a middle-aged Black man from Atlanta decked out in a white Nike tracksuit and Jordans. He returned my goodbye wave with a hearty smile and repeated in his deep Southern accent an adage he'd mentioned earlier that captured the energy of the moment: "The time for Africa is now!"

◆ ◆ ◆

Elsewhere in Ghana, the Year of Return was marked by street fairs in the heart of Accra, a flurry of social media and traditional press, celebrity endorsements, and visits by Steve Harvey, Samuel L. Jackson, and Ludacris, among others. Fairs that took place in the vibrant Osu neighborhood showcased the craftsmanship of local artisans, fashion designers, and chefs in a colorful array of wax print cloth, handmade butters, and prepackaged comfort foods lining Oxford Street—the busiest in Osu.

Fairgoers were mostly first-time travelers or Ghanaian diasporans on holiday visiting family. And this squared with my family members' perception of the festivities. The more I talked with friends and business owners, the more I learned about the largely immaterial effect that the Year of Return was having on the everyday life of local Ghanaians. In fact, my questioning seemed borderline disrespectful to some, who dramatically kissed their teeth and declared that they needed to think about their survival instead of trivial enjoyment.

Locals thought that, at worst, the Year of Return lined the pockets of politicians and, at best, presented diasporans a romanticized portrayal of Ghana with little regard for the challenges of everyday life. The campaign catered to the privileged position of its global audience while largely excluding the country's denizens, and so President Akufo-Addo's international campaign was often brushed off as a marketing ploy to advance his global image.

The people I got to know at CarePoint held similar concerns. CarePoint is an investment holding and advisory company focused on high-growth and impact industry sectors founded by chairman and chief executive officer, Dr. Sangu Delle. I first met Sangu in 2016 at a gathering hosted by a mutual friend during my tenure at Goldman Sachs, and fortuitously our paths would continue to cross over the years. His professional experiences aligned with my study, and he was generous with his limited time, agreeing to meet for interviews whenever he could. He gave me full access to conduct fieldwork at his investment firm, formerly called Golden Palm Investments.[1]

We scheduled our first formal meeting for the beginning of 2019 at Sangu's East Legon company headquarters. I caught an Uber at four p.m., hoping an hour of buffer time would be sufficient. It wasn't. Between traffic and GPS, my driver and I were roaming in circles within feet of Sangu's office and I was more than an hour late. Embarrassed, I hurriedly entered the compound, briefly greeting the dozing security guard seated in the parking lot. I explained the reason for my visit and tardiness to the receptionist, who went to inquire about Sangu's availability without uttering a word. I sat on the vestibule couch fully expecting to be turned away and disappointed by the missed opportunity. It was unclear if I'd get another chance to connect with him in person.

After a couple minutes, the receptionist returned with Sangu in tow. He smiled and said, "The gods must love you today. My meeting was just canceled, so I've got an extra hour!" We laughed as he ushered me into his office, distinguishable by the wooden "CEO" placard bolted to the top of the doorframe. Diplomas and certificates adorned the walls. He took a seat behind his double monitor while gesturing toward the love seat. Cognizant of the time, I sat quickly and clicked on my recorder as Sangu began an oral history of his past. He detailed his lived experience as a cultural mediator between African and American economies. His story reveals the lasting economic legacies of colonialism and proves how race made and continues to make a difference in his participation within capitalism and how that difference informs the more equitable version of capitalism he is building today.

◆ ◆ ◆

Sangu was born into an upper-middle-class family in the Upper West region of Accra where he spent half of his childhood before migrating to the United States. He is the youngest of five children born to his father, a prominent doctor, and stay-at-home mother, whose father was the right-hand man to President Kwame Nkrumah. Capable of reading at the age of two, he was considered a child protégé and identified as special by the headmaster of his nursery school.

"People would call me Opinion 7, which basically means a little kid who thinks he's a grown man. I would show up to my dad's meetings in a full suit and would contribute to the meetings. Usually adults would shut up little kids, but my parents always allowed me to express myself, which most likely had to do with what the nursery teacher told my mom about my academic performance," Sangu reflected. His "very nerdy and weird upbringing" was filled with debates he'd have with his dad about Plato and Nietzsche and recitations of Shakespeare. When he was five, after his father told him that Harvard was a place people go to get "really, really smart," Sangu wrote president David M. Rubenstein to inquire about when he could start school. Eight months later, Sangu got a letter back. President Rubenstein told him that he was too young, but he should keep in touch, which he did over the years. Harvard's president became his pen pal.

Education remained a central focus throughout Sangu's childhood. His mother, a strict disciplinarian, never attended college, which was the biggest regret of her life. It's why she was determined her children would receive the education that she did not. As Sangu put it, "My mom would show up to school *every day,* track my performance *every day,* and talk to *every* teacher *every day.* She was homies with all of them. She knew their birthdays, everything. She was completely involved." Sangu's father was extensively educated and "wrapped up in degrees," unlike his mother. He taught his children the value of a formal education and the importance of saving and money management. Sangu grew up to have what he calls "an insane work ethic, constantly pushing for excellence."

Sangu's financial status changed in the fourth grade when his parents separated. "We went through the bizarre situation of going from high middle class—growing up privileged—to then not having money and living with my mom. I went from having name-brand stuff to my mom buying me fake Adidas. And due to a nasty separation, we hopped around a lot, sometimes living with my mom's friends for days at a time," Sangu recalled. The difficult transition led to multiple fights between Sangu and his mother. "I remember one fight with my mom where she said, 'Get it into your head. You're not rich, you're poor now. Listen, we don't have money.' And in my head I thought, 'Fuck that, I'm not poor.' I hated it every time she said that because to me, poverty is a mindset. I may not have money now, but I am not poor." I questioned what allowed him to believe that was true. "I read a lot. I believe that you create your own future. I was the kid at five who wrote a letter to the president of Harvard because I was told that is where you go to get smart. I just always thought of course what I wanted could happen. I never thought of the issues and obstacles," he replied.

Through his continued correspondence with Harvard, Sangu learned of a summer school program the university hosted for high school seniors. He was a freshman at the time but submitted an application along with his transcript anyway. Harvard admitted him into the program, but now he needed the funds to make the trip across the Atlantic to Boston. Sangu organized a fundraiser in Ghana, going door-to-door raising capital. One memorable donor was the Italian ambassador to Ghana. "He gave me the equivalent of one hundred euros and told me it was immature and foolish for an African boy to think he could get into Harvard," Sangu recalled. "He said even his daughter would not dream about getting in. He offered to use his connections in Italy to see about getting me into a secondary school there but said that Harvard was unrealistic." But Sangu refused to let external opinions determine his trajectory.

During the enrichment program Sangu met students for the first time who attended boarding school. Excited by the concept of school away from home, he applied to some of the most prestigious schools in the United States. He received admittance into all of them, along with full-ride scholarships. He played a game of eenie meenie miney moe to select his new school and home. His pick was the Peddie School in New Jersey—a choice he was pleased with because it was close to New York and he loved the Yankees. Peddie covered the cost of everything except the plane ticket. Instead of running another fundraiser, Sangu made and sold study guides to his classmates for finals, earning him $1,600. He bought a one-way ticket to New Jersey with his earnings. Feeling ashamed of his Ghanaian outfit, he also bought a new Adidas tracksuit and winter gear as soon as he arrived in the States. He blew the remaining $500 on an online auction platform with the hopes of reselling the discounted items he purchased. When the alleged brand-name items finally arrived, he realized they were all fake. "I was devastated, but it was one of my first and biggest lessons in business," he recalled with a grin.

When he found himself in an unfamiliar place with a few quarters to his name, the value of money took on new significance. "Aha-ha, I *knew* I was poor at Peddie," Sangu admitted. I prodded him to share how that knowing squared with his belief that poverty is a mindset. "I grew up in privilege in Ghana," he replied. "My father, a doctor, at the time—let's make up numbers— was making, let's say, $5,000 a year. Let's also say Ghana's GDP per capita at that time is $500 and so my dad is making ten times that. In that context, he's a big baller. In the United States, he is so poor he would qualify for every single government assistance. He'd be living in an insane amount of poverty." Sangu went on to compare his experience at Peddie with that of his peers. His classmates would go out to eat, which he could never afford to do. He'd get rice from the Chinese restaurant nearby for a dollar and beg the waitress to give him the hot chili sauce for free. His friend Nana Kwesi lived nearby, and Nana's family gave him permission to raid their kitchen whenever he needed to. He filled up his sack with canned tuna and corned beef from their pantry before returning to Peddie. He'd then mix the tuna and corned beef into the hot chili sauce to make a stew that he ate with the dollar rice. Those were the better days.

There was a time when Sangu had no money to do laundry, so he took a bar of soap and started washing his clothes in the bathroom sink. His friend Sean walked in and quickly interceded once he realized what Sangu was doing. "Oh, Sangu, no, that's not how you do it!" Sean said as he put Sangu's clothes in the washer and reached into his pocket for quarters to start the machine. Sangu didn't let on he knew how to work a washer. Instead he said, "Oh, okay. . . . I see. So how does the dryer work?"

"I didn't give a fuck about my economic difference or how it came across to others. I was in America. I was in school for *free*!" he recalled. People would complain about the food at school, but all Sangu could think about was that the food was free. "I'm in a school that costs $60,000 a year . . . for *free*!" He took five Advanced Placement (AP) courses one year and six the next, and he had to get the dean's approval since most students took only two at a time. Sangu was hell-bent on taking advantage of everything. He was at every free event and signed up for everything he could. "In Ghana, to get Bourdieusian for a minute," he said, referring to the French sociologist Pierre Bourdieu, "where I didn't have financial capital, I was very aware of my social and cultural capital, even though I didn't know it was called that. I had and deployed it enormously." In the United States, he had no capital of any form. Sangu was broke across the board and was forced to look at life from that perspective to create solutions.

Sangu made extra cash by working at Peddie's Alumni Center and starting a resale clothing company with a business partner based in London. He capitalized on an opportunity to make money selling American brands in London, where they were difficult to acquire. He'd take the Greyhound bus to Washington, D.C., purchase Timberland shoes and other in-demand fashion pieces, and ship them to his partner. From there his partner would resell the items, generating a return on their investment. He did all of this while taking a record number of AP courses and founding a nonprofit called Clean Water, an organization that provided access to clean water to those living in West Africa. "I was always trying to figure out some kind of hustle," he explained.

Peddie exposed Sangu to unseen wealth, but his enrollment at Harvard was the next level of access to the world of the financial elite. He learned that being smart gave him currency as he acquired social and cultural capital, but doing so came with challenges. He knew people thought his admittance was because of his Blackness. One night Sangu and his roommate Jeremy, who would go on to raise $100 million by his late twenties and manage over half a billion dollars in assets at one of Wall Street's most respected hedge funds, were having a conversation about a student from Jeremy's high school who went to Oxford after scoring perfect marks in nine AP courses, setting the record at Hotchkiss. Sangu was unimpressed. "I got perfect scores in eleven APs in two years," he replied. "Impossible," Jeremy rebutted. Sangu pulled up his results on the College Board, which left Jeremy's jaw hanging. Their relationship was forever changed. From then on Jeremy would invite Sangu to events. If his parents were visiting town, he'd ask Sangu to join them for lunch. Jeremy treated him differently, better even. "Being able to say I have perfect scores on eleven APs meant something to these white people," Sangu said.

But Sangu didn't care about Jeremy's change in perspective or treatment. His rationale was: "This guy is a billionaire. He's looking down on me because he thinks I have nothing to offer. But I am so smart he is forced to recognize me." Jeremy knew a lot about finance and was often trading during class. "So on the left hand, yes, it sucked he said 'impossible' and didn't believe at face value I could get eleven perfect scores. But on the other hand, he was the smartest person I knew in finance at the time and I had a lot to learn from him. For me, the right hand wins. I wanted to soak up everything."

Sangu enrolled in Economics 101 and fell in love with macroeconomics. "The world of finance sounded exciting and glamorized. They made it seem like you're controlling all this capital, and the idea was that finance controls the world. I found it all intellectually interesting," he recounted. Eager to put theory to practice, Sangu applied for summer internships at every leading investment bank. He was rejected from every bank, despite exceptional grades and an impressive résumé. So he put his social capital to work in a last-ditch effort. With the help of a Harvard alum, he secured an internship at Bear Stearns in 2007.

The summer of 2007 was crazy, Sangu said. It's when Bear Stearns collapsed due to the subprime mortgage crisis. And Sangu had a front seat to the madness as an analyst in the hedge fund division. Bear Stearns paid him time and a half for overtime, so Sangu would report to work at five a.m. and leave at midnight. His first paycheck was more than $3,000, which was cause for celebration. Sangu and his buddies walked to a bar in Midtown where he bought drinks and shots for the entire bar. Afterward they went to a jewelry store where they all bought watches. He laughed recalling the memory and relating it to the Kanye West rap lyric: "I rather buy eighty gold chains and go ig'nant. I know Spike Lee gon' kill me." He worked for ten weeks and made around $33,000. He'd never seen so much money.

He was hooked after that summer. During internships at Goldman Sachs and Morgan Stanley, he began building the concept for his venture Golden Palm Investments (GPI). "I had all these ideas about Ghana and finance, and I would talk about it for a while until eventually, Jeremy was like, 'Just go do it and raise capital,'" he said. Sangu searched through files on his computer to show me his first GPI pitch deck, clicking through the slides with nostalgia. Raising capital for his venture was "a whole education," he recalled. "I didn't know people would give me money to materialize my ideas!" He raised $50,000 among his classmates and invested in West African agriculture and cattle arbitrage after noticing a lucrative opportunity in the supply-chain process. Sangu chose to juggle managing GPI with his burgeoning Wall Street career because he believed he'd make the leap to full-time entrepreneurship one day. "I didn't know when the cutoff would be for my time on Wall Street, but I knew I would use the skills I gained there to build my own business."

Sangu spent his summer at Goldman Sachs in the firm's Special Situations Group (SSG). He coined it the "Navy SEALs of the investment bank," an elite and exclusive group responsible for bringing in a significant portion of the firm's profits at the time. "All the white guys had no idea how I got in, but SSG didn't care about affirmative action," he said. "All it cared about was making money, so it shifted how people saw us. That time was the cockiest I ever was, and in hindsight, I knew nothing. I was just so excited and felt on top of the world. I lived in Brooklyn, rented a brownstone . . . life was phenomenal."

In 2008 Goldman Sachs maintained a strong brand perception and was unfazed by the crisis. "In fact, Goldman made money during the crisis," Sangu recounted. He felt proud to be interning at an organization that boasted collaboration and excellence despite apprehension about public criticism of Goldman Sachs's role in the Great Recession. "All that mattered was the numbers you put up. They romanticized everything. Later, when I started working in the industry full-time, I realized that race, sex, gender, relationships, and political alignments matter."

Sangu grew disenchanted the more time he spent in the industry. He entered the field thinking he was making an impact but realized he "wasn't doing shit." Sangu's ideal and the reality of Wall Street were colliding. He saw the "darkness of finance" through the trading floor—the "stereotypical, macho, alpha male behavior and personality" that makes films like the *Wolf of Wall Street* more relatable than not. The culture was eat or be eaten, kill or be killed. "Everything was about money, which came across in the language you would hear and the way people would talk. I remember a managing director who told me his family life sucks. His kids hated him, and the only reason his wife stuck around was because he buys her what she wants. I just thought it all sounded very dark," Sangu recalled.

He didn't feel the need to be an asshole like his male colleagues, but he felt the pressure of the cultural norms and what's required to build social and cultural capital on the trading floor. "If you're the guy whose jokes are all goody-two-shoes and not the regular sexist jokes, no one is rooting for you and saying you're their boy when your name comes up for a bonus," he explained. The people who build personal relationships, no matter the cost, are the ones who get rewarded. People made insensitive comments daily. But the question Sangu had to ask himself was, "Do you want to be the guy that polices that?" As a man of faith who religiously carried a rosary in his pocket, Sangu was bombarded with colleagues "talking shit about faith." He'd push the rosary deeper into his pocket, praying it wouldn't come out each time someone made a callous remark. He couldn't help but think, "These guys decide my bonus."

Sangu's playbook to success on the trading floor was to keep his head down and do his work. His approach would have been different if he planned to stay at the firm long term. "Ultimately, there's a cost to speaking up, and I just always had to measure and ensure it was worth it," he reasoned.

◆ ◆ ◆

Sangu was completely disillusioned by finance after another internship and full-time employment at Morgan Stanley. He considered different industries and a permanent move back to Ghana. Glancing at the Harvard alumni Facebook page, he stumbled upon a job advertisement posted by a hedge fund founder who was hiring private equity analysts in its San Francisco office to support venture capital work in emerging markets.

Sangu was skeptical, but he was persuaded by friends to chat with Chris Hansen, the founder of Valiant. He flew to California and was glad he did. "Chris saved finance for me. I loved the guy and the culture of his firm. He taught me that you don't have to be an asshole, you don't have to be dark. You can be socially impact focused. The values of the firm were different and inspiring," he said. After a refreshing two years at Valiant working in long and short global equities, private equity, and venture capital, Sangu returned to Harvard to complete his MBA and JD. He had plans to scale up his own firm in Ghana.

Sangu's thesis about sub-Saharan Africa was the catalyst for GPI's creation. He believed that the continent would develop into an attractive place for investment based on industry trends that pointed toward poststructural adjustments to the economy, political stability, and the growth of a consumer class. "The idea was that there would be opportunities to invest in this development wave similar to what we saw happen in India and China in the emerging world," he declared. Sangu scaled the business from investing in agriculture and cow arbitrage to venture investments in the technology industry. "We said we are going to find the best tech firms across Africa and back them," he asserted. The approach was simple yet sophisticated: Create a concentrated portfolio, which meant fewer investments but extensive due diligence, to make multiple investments to select companies for the long term.

Instead of one hundred companies, his portfolio would hold fewer than twenty. GPI would get up to one thousand ideas a year and only seriously review one hundred. Of that, he'd take ten to the investment committee for investment in one to three companies. GPI would invest anything from $100,000 to a few million dollars into a company. With exceptional ventures, GPI would invest even more. What determined GPI's investment in a company was the strength of its team, addressable market size, return on investment, a risk evaluation, and confidence in the company's ability to execute.

Over time, GPI's operational division, headquartered in Ghana, built a real estate, financial services, and healthcare business designed to create value for the African consumer. The healthcare business spun into CarePoint, where Sangu spends most of his time acquiring healthcare assets across the continent. "Why the emphasis on healthcare?" I asked.

"Because it ticks all the boxes. I grew up around healthcare, so I have an affinity toward it. It's also the most interesting intersection of risk and reward, impact, opportunity to build an extraordinary business, and most importantly, ability to scale in a Pan-African way."

I let our conversation linger on Sangu's practice of Pan-Africanism.

"I grew up drinking the Pan-African Kool-Aid," he joked while searching the photo gallery on his iPhone. He showed me a picture of Kwame Nkrumah, one of the forefathers of Pan-Africanism, standing next to his maternal grandmother and grandfather. His grandfather was responsible for establishing Nkrumah's first Bureau of Military Counterintelligence, and his grandmother for the marriage between Nkrumah and Fathia Rizk, who was Egyptian. "At an early age I was introduced to the idea that the destiny of all Black people—African and African diasporic—are linked together. So there has always been that emotional, personal tie to the continent for me," he reflected, his eyes fixed on the image he held in his hands.

Sangu is a staunch believer that practicing Pan-Africanism can create unseen economic and political leverage for the fifty-four countries that make up Africa. He made the case with a compelling example: "Take Sierra Leone or Liberia. Both have tiny population sizes. You can't really build a sizable market. But when you think about it from a Pan-African perspective, that's one billion–plus people. That gives you a size to then rival China, India, and some of those other large markets. And, of course, we're talking about fifty-four countries, so there is great complexity, but that's why things like the Africa Free Trade Agreement comes into play to account for the complexity." The African Continental Free Trade Area (AfCFTA) is the world's largest trade area in terms of country members, bringing them into a single, liberalized market. "The more we can move toward a harmonized continental market, the more it gives us massive scale," Sangu explained. "Geopolitically, if Ghana is negotiating against the European Union, there's a limit to what Ghana can extract in terms of value. But if the African Union is representing fifty-four African countries, two trillion dollars, and a billion people, it's a different bargaining situation."

There are clear geopolitical advantages to Pan-Africanism. As power is accumulated, the more powerful the people on the continent become. "If Black purchasing power can move with one voice," Sangu said, "it suddenly has tremendous economic power." And the African diaspora plays a critical role in this process. The remittances of diasporans are a large market and funder of economic activity on the continent. In 2023 alone, migrant workers remitted $95 billion to their communal networks in Africa.[2] One way Sangu's firm is leveraging this power is through the development of a product akin to health insurance. The diasporan pays a monthly fee, and physicians on the ground conduct regular checkups on family members and provide access to the best medical care.

Our conversation led us to Sangu's ethos for creating business standards and managing the cultural conflicts that arise during international commerce. Sangu handles these challenges by encouraging his team to understand the why. He used to impose strict governance standards that mirrored those of the United States, but that created problems because the standards were foreign to his team. Taking the time to educate and build awareness about investor needs helped his team know that he, in his words, "wasn't trying to be a dick," but instead mitigating potential risks if the business did not meet global standards. "You're thinking about it in an American way," was the common response from his team. But taking the extra time to inform his staff on why he made certain decisions helped them appreciate his choices as well as show him where he needed to change his approach.

An "initiative I wanted to introduce was equity stakes in the business for employees. That got pushback," he said. The experiences forced him to take a step back and learn what mattered to his employees. "People didn't give a shit. They don't care about equity. In the United States, you cannot have a startup without offering equity. But I had to learn that people don't care about that. Their thinking was: 'You're going to pay me my bonus. And I want my bonus in cash.'" Physical compensation was important, as were other things like promotional titles and parties. Certain corporate concepts that do well in the United States didn't have the same appeal in Ghana.

Uncertainty was Sangu's hypothesis as to why. He knew if he built a business in San Francisco, people would understand the importance of equity as part of the reward structure. "On the

Ghana side, they're looking at it like: 'Look, this guy is going to give me a quarter of a percent in this business. Excuse my French, but what the fuck does that mean for me?' To them, they're not seeing the value. Whereas, if you pay me a bonus of a thousand dollars, that's a thousand dollars in my pocket," he reasoned. The concept that a quarter of a percent may be worth $20,000 in the future was esoteric. It wasn't the norm and created more questions than answers when what his team knew and trusted was cash. Why? Because the state of Ghana's infrastructure does not yet inspire people to believe in corporate promises of future compensation. Tangible and immediate cash is valued most because it requires people and organizations to stay true to their word in a society where so many bear the negative consequences of systemic corruption and greed.

The cultural conflicts were domestic too. Sangu held more "progressive ideas" than others on his team. They didn't have the experience of spending half of their life in America, and it showed. "I once implemented a Me Too campaign in the office with roundtable discussions and talks, which caused tension and people didn't understand it," he recalled.

Sangu figured out other things employees cared about, like training opportunities outside the country, and used them to incentivize excellence. His attention to the desires of his employees and workplace culture reveals his intentional and nuanced practice of capitalism as an entrepreneur, including the investment in both inputs (the company's people) and outputs (execution of the company's mission and international reception) that is required to create an ecosystem that nurtures social good for employees, consumers, and stakeholders. Sangu's identity as a Black business owner of an Africa-based company with a global vision reveals the unique duality of having to manage internal, corporate expectations built on African culture, while disrupting Western perceptions about the viability and vitality of African business. Not only is he an entrepreneur, but he is also a mediator between two cultures that instinctively clash.

I'd spend the next two years observing his team, but for now my borrowed hour with Sangu was up. He was flying to New York that evening for a board meeting, so we agreed to meet in person either in Brooklyn, our shared second home, or once more in Ghana—whichever came first.

◆ ◆ ◆

I wanted to see the effects of Black Capitalism on Sangu's staff, including how their beliefs or behaviors changed—or not—because of Sangu's vision for how to do business. I returned to the East Legon office later that week.

Most days were slow, with little to interrupt the mundane nature of cubicle work. But what stood out was the small talk made in passing between employees. They'd crack jokes, show interest in one another's family members, and share ideas they were developing to aid efficiency in business operations. Everyone prepared their pitches for the management team in the hopes of increasing their chances of winning the Employee of the Year Award announced at the annual Christmas party. A golden framed headshot of the firm's current Employee of the Year hung in the vestibule for all to see, and people would glance at the picture and debate who deserved the award this year.

My presence was a distraction regardless of how open staff were to sacrificing work time to talk to me. But one person who took me under her wing was Maame. She had studied business administration and management at one of Ghana's top universities and applied for a job at GPI after listening to Sangu present a guest lecture at her school. Inspired by his story, she was eager to join the team and acquire the skills needed to deepen her knowledge of investing, business development, and marketing. She joined GPI in 2015, and her charismatic spirit and natural inclination to help others quickly made her indispensable.

On occasions when Maame had time to spare during her lunch break, we'd chat about our food startups, her passion for baking, and her dreams to scale her business one day. She also gave me a crash course on her daily work streams and how she conducted due diligence on the companies that submitted pitch proposals to the firm.

She told me she felt empowered in her role as an investment analyst and proud to work at a place that made money by making other people's lives better. I wondered if her glowing reviews of GPI were exaggerated to protect herself from an outsider who was also a friend of her boss. I expected people who spoke to me to exercise discretion, but as the months went on, I grew convinced that Maame's passion for her job was true.

She'd tell me stories about GPI's early days and her role in building the firm with the management team and watching the business evolve over time. "It started with long nights, many overnighters, and lots and lots of work," she laughingly said. "The closeness that I witnessed between colleagues was established during those overnighters, which created a familial culture." But over time, as the firm grew more profitable and increased its headcount to satisfy business needs, the company culture shifted. "If there was one piece of critical feedback I'd give is that with the growth came building renovations, the separate offices and cubicles, which has made it difficult to engage with others the way we once did. It's something I miss," she shared. Sitting together in her office, which could fit an eight-foot folding table and not much else, she talked about how employees had to be more intentional about building relationships because of the built environment.

One tradition the firm continues is a book club, where once a week an employee is tasked with presenting a piece of media that is important to them at the morning meeting. Maame recalled Sangu's presentation as especially memorable because of its vulnerability. He screened his TED Talk on mental health, in which he reflects on a debilitating anxiety attack he experienced as a result of tremendous stress and the shame of not feeling comfortable to share what he was going through with anyone. "I felt suffocated by the rigid architecture of our African masculinity. . . . Come down with pneumonia and your mother will rush you to the nearest hospital for medical treatment. But dare to declare depression, and your local pastor will be driving out demons and blaming witches in your village," Sangu said.[3] His talk on mental health illuminated a taboo topic throughout Africa.

We volleyed ideas back and forth as Maame daydreamed about which text she'd choose to present when her turn came. Despite Sangu's demanding schedule, which kept him out of the office for days at a time, he was insistent on always being present for the presentations to ensure his staff knew how important they were to him. The book club was an initiative team members looked forward to in their hopes to build community and expand working relationships into the personal sphere.

Why was this? Because people want to be seen in their full humanity rather than just as laborers. Despite corporate appeals to "bring your whole self to work," many are conditioned to do the exact opposite—leaving their whole self at the revolving door from fear of retribution. Professionals—Black or otherwise—rationalize the contradiction as corporate antics and resign themselves to the belief that this way of working is the most we can hope for. Though we are trained to show up as less than our full selves, it can be mentally, emotionally, and physically taxing to bifurcate ourselves in this way. Many of us spend more time at work and with colleagues than we do with loved ones and our chosen communities. No matter where they exist around the world, workplace cultures that genuinely invite and accommodate people in their full humanity while maintaining the safety and respect of all employees are not only welcomed but also needed so that we can disavow ourselves of the misconception that there is an actual distinction between work and life. People often believe that they either "live to work" or "work to live." Here's a third option: Live to live. One aspect of living this human experience is that working should deepen our exploration with ourselves instead of producing a stifled expression within us. Today, the ability to bring one's full self to work is a privilege that requires access to the kind of power and influence that overrides the threat of penalty or organizational leadership that is invested in the lives of its people, not its laborers.

Capitalism as we know it makes profit to the bottom line of any corporation. But seemingly insignificant initiatives like the company's book club inspired courageous conversations and connection, which allowed people to feel valued not just as employees but, more important, as people. Such practices of capitalism prioritize both profit and social good.

◆ ◆ ◆

As the highly anticipated Christmas party grew near, I was excited when Sangu extended me an invite. The venue was Little Fingers, a popular restaurant in East Legon. I wore a green-and-red mud cloth dress for the festive occasion. On my short walk to the entrance from where my Uber driver had dropped me, I ran into Sangu, who was dressed in a crisp gray-and-black kaftan and standing in the middle of the road. As I got closer I realized he was preoccupied with a phone call that seemed work related, given his matter-of-fact tone. "Make yourself comfortable, I'm right behind you," he said, holding the phone against his chest as we exchanged waves. It'd been weeks since I last saw him in person.

I picked a seat at one of the outdoor tables adorned in bright green-and-yellow tablecloths set up specifically for the gathering. Sangu reappeared, took a seat next to me, and introduced me to members of his team I'd heard of but never met in person. I met his head of finance; the chief executive officer of Robito, GPI's newly acquired healthcare clinic; and other senior leaders. Guests sat next to colleagues within their business lines (e.g., finance, healthcare, operations), which created distinct boundaries in the open seating arrangement. I laughed to myself as I realized I was in the finance section, having been drawn to the people I recognized from the office.

The party was supposed to start at seven p.m., but like most Ghanaian social affairs, it began late: Sangu kicked off the celebration with welcoming remarks at nine. He used a portable microphone to project his voice across the four hundred feet of outdoor space that contained nine round tables full of guests. Sangu noted the African excellence each employee embodied, the firm's execution of its key performance indicators, and his expectations for 2020. "Together we will soar to new heights," he said with conviction.

I looked at the crowd of melanated faces that were smiling and nodding in agreement. The team took pride in their work because they knew it was making a difference in people's lives. Edem, the firm's marketing and social media analyst who was crouched next to me taking photos, leaned in and whispered, "I've never worked at a place like this before." A place that cared about the well-being of its employees, changing the economic position of Africans around the world, and its bottom line.

Sangu concluded his remarks with the highly anticipated reveal of the Employee of the Year Award. But before he named the winner, he talked about the value of the women on the GPI team. He even poked fun at the men on the team who made friendly jokes about "needing men's rights because women's rights were taking over." Seeing men and women laughing with one another at Sangu's comments proved that Sangu's efforts to tackle uncomfortable topics like gender equality in Africa were beginning to make a difference. Even though his large-scale #MeToo initiative was too American to be successful in a Ghanaian context (at least for now), the smaller acts of interculturalism had an impact.

Everyone listened in rapt attention for who would take home the coveted plaque and the hundreds of dollars of prize money Sangu held in his left hand. "The Employee of the Year is the quintessential team player, always ready and willing to lend a helping hand and further the mission of the business. She is a person who embodies what GPI is all about. This year's employee of the year award goes to . . . Maame!" Everyone cheered as Maame, shocked and speechless, slowly walked toward Sangu to accept her award. Stumbling over her words, Maame thanked the management team for recognizing her efforts and everyone else for making GPI "her home" especially in times when she felt it was her only one.

A swarm of female colleagues rushed Maame with hugs and words of praise. Now that the announcements were over, the party could get started. Restaurant staff carried out large, sterling silver heating trays filled with banku, fried chicken and fish, jollof and vegetable fried rice, and okra stew. It was second nature for Maame and a handful of women to crowd behind the buffet table to serve people.

With empty plates in hand, team members formed a line that wrapped along the perimeter of the patio space and the connected parking lot. Sangu left his seat to recruit men to help Maame and the others serve guests. He did this until there was an equal gender distribution of servers. Returning to our table, he talked about the "cultural readjustments" he makes like this one to continue the slow yet steady uptick in changed behaviors of his team.

At eleven p.m. the master of ceremonies, who doubled as the disc jockey, invited guests who were now full and tired to a dance competition. Each table was tasked with selecting a representative to dance for the chance to win two thousand cedis (the equivalent of two hundred dollars). Some took the game seriously, busting out their flyest breakdancing moves. Others, visibly embarrassed, giggled their way through their five-minute showcase. When it was time to select the winner, voters showed their loyalty to their representative rather than the dancer with the greatest skill. Sangu immediately adjusted the voting rules to account for merit rather than allegiance. The competition revived the energy of the group as some people got up to dance, others circled back to the buffet line where Maame chose to stay, and still others arrived fashionably late to the party.

Hours passed and the party kept on. People were happy to celebrate the end of a successful fiscal year and enjoy one another's company. Colleagues-turned-friends chatted about their holiday travel plans, Detty December (a festive period at the end of the year marked by high energy and optimism) parties they looked forward to, and Year of Return news. People were merry, but Sangu's attention was fixed to his phone as he executed one final deal before offices closed for the holidays. "You're the only one here working," I said with curiosity as I watched him take a bite of the fried red snapper on his plate.

"I'm always working and no one else is, but this way, at least they are able to enjoy themselves," he said, turning his gaze to the people on the dance floor in the middle of a choreographed dance move. "I get paid more than anyone else, so the brunt of the responsibility falls on my shoulders, not on theirs."

Just as he said this the power shut off, casting the immediate neighborhood into utter darkness. A low hum replaced the Burna Boy record that had been blaring through the six-foot-tall speakers on the patio. Everyone returned to their seats both laughing and criticizing Ghana's "light off" problem.[4] They'd sit and hope for the power supply to come back on. Sangu rose from his chair and sprang into action, disappearing into the back of the restaurant to inquire about a backup generator. He only returned to the group when the lights flickered on and Burna Boy's voice rang out from the speakers.

It was nearly two a.m. when I departed, the first to leave the function. People continued to spill in as Club beers were snapped open and the DJ spun his tracks. From the parking lot where I waited for my Uber, I turned to take a final look at the gathering. Sangu's opening remarks about GPI being a place of family and belonging was on display as I caught glimpses of intimate exchanges between people whose bonds with one another extended beyond the walls of GPI. The hidden, marginal undercommons that signifies Black community-making on Wall Street was not present here. The commons of GPI was center stage for inclusive connection and fugitive planning.

The GPI staff mirrored the Pan-African unity Sangu is working to build across the continent; he built a team aligned in their strategic engagement in capitalism to produce opportunities for global Black social, political, and economic thriving.

It's important to remember that Blackness is both a racial identity and a social position. To be Black is to be the "other," or a deviation from the socially accepted norm. In an African context where most people look like one another, GPI team members weren't troubled with navigating *inter*racial relations among one another. Everyone identified as a Black African. Instead, their shared work product doubled as a challenge to enduring (neo)colonial perceptions that Africa is a place for resource extraction and disinvestment because of who lives on the continent. The GPI team's expression of Black capitalism serves notice on long-standing global beliefs about the social standing and economic potential of Black Africans on the continent.

Our lived experiences are interconnected whether we realize it or not. When Sangu regularly travels to America to run board meetings, broker deals, and generate CarePoint buy-in, he's representing not only himself but also his team, the companies they invest in, and the people they service throughout Africa, all of whom are out of sight and mind for many of us here in America.

Sangu's professional presence in the United States challenges Western beliefs that Africa's economic problems and promise are its own to deal with. His bridging of the two worlds and their respective cultures forces us to reckon with the effects of American (neo)colonialism in Africa, and engage with cultural mediators like Sangu who refuse to ignore Africa's troubled history, shaped in part by Western influence. The Pan-African vision he has for Africa requires the participation of people from across the world. Sangu's story is a reminder that we've inherited, and are all responsible for, our imperfect economic system, whose reach extends beyond the geographic boundaries of what we consider home.

CHAPTER 10

An African Renaissance

As the Year of Return ended, celebrities flooded the country. Accra was abuzz as news outlets shared the latest to land at Kotoka International Airport. T.I., Rick Ross, Lupita Nyong'o, Boris Kodjoe, Beyoncé, and Jay-Z were just a few to visit and receive private tours of the country. Bozoma "BadAssBoz" Saint John, a proud Ghanaian and C-suite executive, and Boris Kodjoe hosted the *Essence* Full Circle Festival, an invitation-only experience of Ghanaian history and culture that was publicly supported by President Akufo-Addo. Footage of high-profile attendees participating in the private festival made its way through social media, driving public opinion that Ghana was the place to be. It was a historic moment.

I didn't have access to the festival, which included a trip to Cape Coast Castle, priority seating, perks at music festivals, and an economic forum about the role of the diaspora in the development of Africa. But I did attend a star-studded Studio 189 event, thanks to a chance meeting with Abrima, one of the cofounders (the other is Rosario Dawson), at an NYC birthday party, during a quick reprieve from months of fieldwork. Based in Ghana, Studio 189 is a social enterprise that promotes and curates African fashion. Days before the brand's event, Abrima put out a call for volunteers to offer support with a day of preparations. I happily volunteered since I figured doing so would get me research access to some of the elite diasporans.

I arrived at the multipurpose space tucked away in Osu on a late morning five days before the end of the year. The renovated single-story house painted in white with a wooden "Studio 189" sign tacked above the front door sat on a spacious compound with shiny green grass and a weeping willow tree that towered above the gate walls. Someone had built a creative photo op at the end of the gravel parking lot: a ten-foot wall covered with multiple shreds of colorful batik textiles that glimmered in the smoldering sun. The concept for the day's festivities was an immersive multimodal experience for guests, and offerings included yoga on the shaded lawn, batik textile printing, an indoor photo gallery viewing, and the main attraction—a Year of Return panel.

Along with other volunteers, I scrambled to source mats for the Vinyasa yoga session, measured and hung portraits of Abrima and Rosario around the living room and kitchen space, and arranged valet parking for notable guests. All the hired support staff were young male laborers from the area, and I was curious to know what they thought of the Year of Return events, including this one. As the group took a twenty-minute break to refuel on the Eddy's cheese pizzas Abrima had ordered, I broached the topic.

George rolled his eyes dismissively. He was the eighteen-year-old alpha male of the group and had referred to me as a "chick" hours before when complaining to his boss about Abrima's instructions to listen to me as we built an outdoor fixture. "Year of Return? What is that?" The others laughed and nodded in agreement, with one adding, "I came to chop money. This Year of Return you speak of, I don't know, ooo." I shut up about the matter as their collective opinion was made clear. They were there to work, collect their money, and leave. Anything beyond that was irrelevant, especially the lives of elites who would enjoy the fruits of their labor.

The event's start went smoothly as guests trickled in, simultaneously networking while moseying their way through the activities. Thirty minutes before the panel was to begin, Abrima approached me with an update at the house gates, where I was checking Eventbrite tickets. One of the panelists had missed his flight. "Since you're a scholar and entrepreneur, do you want to take his place and draft up a few questions to facilitate the panel discussion?" she asked. I agreed to write some questions, but I was terrified by the thought of being on the panel. I didn't know what I could say that would matter to anyone.

But after much prodding, I reluctantly sat next to Abrima, Nigerian-born actor Samuel Adegoke, and the Ugandan American Black travel influencer Jessica Nabongo on a raised bench underneath the weeping willow tree. Guests gathered around, taking seats on the colorful yoga mats left behind from the afternoon's session.

How does our African identity show up in the work that we do? What is the value of Africa's cultural currency today and how have you witnessed it change over time? How do we capitalize on the fact that all eyes are on Africa in a new way for the first time since centuries of exploitation and excavation of African resources? These were some of the tough questions Abrima directed to the panelists. Audience members chimed in occasionally with their own insights and questions. The conversation ended with a final question from a middle-aged Puerto Rican man: "What does it mean to be Pan-African and how can we apply it in this moment?" We sat silent for a moment as the gravity of his question dawned on all of us.

A lanky man with ebony skin who was laid out belly-flat on a blue-and-white straw mat piped up in response: "One of our founding fathers, Kwame Nkrumah, once said, 'I am not African because I was born in Africa but because Africa was born in me.' When the Year of Return is over and most of us leave for our other homes across the diaspora, I think it's our responsibility to take back this moment to the communities we are a part of and share with them the potential and promise of the continent so they feel included in this moment."

Listeners snapped their fingers in agreement. Abrima turned the mic back to the panelists one last time as she asked us for any parting words. The other two made points about the importance of supporting local businesses and educating oneself on the culture and history of Ghana and Africa to ensure experiences are informed by facts. Still thinking about the Puerto Rican man's question and George's flippant comment from earlier, I challenged the group to consider what it means to be Pan-African while *in* Ghana, and to recognize the privilege inherent in our ability to attend Studio 189's swanky event.

I warned against practicing a false kind of African unity that exacerbates the disconnect between the diasporan experience and the local, everyday lives of those who maintain a country whose resurgence narrative leaves them largely unaccounted for.

"Shoulda kept your mouth shut. Here we go again," I thought to myself, seeing the blank faces that followed my parting comment. I worried I had killed the mood, immediately regretting my decision to speak on the panel.

The feeling of awkwardness and discomfort I sensed in that moment was the same feeling I observed when my colleague told me "Black Capitalists don't exist" during my presentation at Yale. In both moments, I felt I had said something radical and unwelcome in a space that ironically considers itself progressive. My gentle reminder, to Yale's Black Studies Department and a fashion house in Accra, was that we all have responsibility and agency in creating the kind of world we want to live in. What will get us there is vision and ambition coupled with collective and pragmatic thinking. But as guests lingered to chat, I was reassured that my comments inspired thoughtfulness as people approached me with stories about their aspirations to build social and cultural ties through their local investment endeavors. Their dreams not only to return home but also to stay and participate in the local economy in ways that produced profitable outcomes, collective economic security, and community read of a new kind of capitalism from which we can all learn.

From the corner of my eye I could see volunteers transforming the space for the after party as the DJ carried out his turntable and the sponsored bar was filled with liquor and local beers and lagers like Club, Star, and Stone. Exhausted by the full day, I opted to head home and quietly slipped past the guarded gate before turning the corner onto the main road where my Uber ride was waiting for me. There I ran into George. He was visibly fatigued while directing traffic into the designated valet area. We locked eyes from across the street and I waved goodbye as he said in response, "See you, Naa-Du."

◆ ◆ ◆

I woke up to the cock's crow at 5:25 a.m. the next day, anxious to get a start on my morning preparations for AfroFuture—Kelewele's debut in the African market. On the day I launched Kelewele, I promised myself that I would build a business that was attached to its source. The thought of sharing Kelewele exclusively in an American market felt neglectful of the people and culture that produced it in the first place. I wanted Kelewele to be a bridge between cultures, and so I needed to open both ends of that bridge. Excited by the prospect of bringing my business back to its roots, yet clueless about how to do so effectively, I leaned on friends who connected me with restaurateurs in Accra who helped me source commercial kitchen equipment and space, and navigate the tricky business terrain as a diasporan.

"If you can pull it off here, you can pull it off anywhere," was a word of both caution and encouragement from people in the local food industry. What they knew, which I didn't yet, was how daily price hikes in the cost of goods, broken supply chains, frequent power outages, and an unreliable and inaccessible labor market make it exceptionally difficult for entrepreneurs to build food businesses that both turn a profit and generate enough income to live off comfortably. My experience in America had spoiled me. I'd learn that the effort and the social capital needed to pull off a one-day event in Accra were greater than those needed for any multiday festival I'd ever done in America. The obstacles between a Black entrepreneur and their success were stacked even higher here.

Pulling into El Wak Stadium at nine a.m. in a battered blue minitruck carrying a two-hundred-pound freezer full of assorted plantain ice creams, I did not know what to expect. The AfroFuture team scurried about while the food vendors organized their ten-by-ten-foot huts made from wood and straw and painted over in loud colors shaped into Adinkra symbols. Surprisingly, the owners of the business to the right of my stall were also my Brooklyn neighbors.

We'd never met one another before, but as we chatted, I learned that their flagship café, as well as their home, was two blocks away from the apartment I lived in at the time. AfroFuture inspired the couple's first business trip to Ghana and their plans to relocate permanently. In front of us, a team of fifteen chefs in yellow aprons, who were managed by a Ghanaian friend of mine who also lived in Brooklyn, were cooking something historic—a three-ton pot of jollof rice—the largest ever in the world.

As the gates opened a few hours later and ushered in thousands of festivalgoers, I was amazed to see so many people I recognized from my Brooklyn community in Accra, including former Goldman Sachs colleagues. "All of Brooklyn is in Ghana!" was the running joke of the day as friends would stop by, enjoy some plantain ice cream as a reprieve from the heat, and share the highlights of their trip. I bounced back and forth between pitching Kelewele to curious consumers and talking about investment ideas with diasporans who wanted to know how I applied my business interest to the Ghanaian market. Some wanted to get into shea butter exportation, others wanted to deal in textile and fashion, and most were interested in land acquisition. I shared my own vision for Kelewele in Ghana: to build an end-to-end global supply chain for plantain exportation sustained by plantain farms developed by local farmers paid respectable wages. I wanted grocery shoppers around the world to pick up a plantain and read "Grown in Ghana" on the sticker to inspire thoughtfulness about international food networks and the people who create them. And I told my listeners about the work I'd started to build a boutique, beachfront vegan resort that offers both locals and tourists a restorative experience that is culturally relevant, health-forward, and accessible. "The real estate and hospitality industry is ruthless, I'm learning. But how cool would it be to have a unique and immersive foodie experience that is sustainable and strengthens the community you're a part of? That's why I keep at it. Plus, my family is here. Which means part of my mind is always here, as I'm constantly thinking about how I can invest my time and resources here too," I said as travelers asked me my reason for pursuing this massive undertaking while living stateside.

I scooped the last bit of Liquid Gold plantain ice cream (made with actual gold dust in recognition of Ghana's former name, the Gold Coast) at 12:11 a.m. Fighting sleep as I slumped on top of the lowboy freezer, I waited in the hut, lit by a single lightbulb, for the owner of the blue minitruck to return. It was a successful day for Kelewele. But the value of AfroFuture for the hundreds of people I encountered was the opportunity to network and share resources to maintain the momentum beyond this Year of Return.

◆ ◆ ◆

I slept in the next morning and woke to the sound of my phone ringing. Wemimo was in town for forty-eight hours, so we made plans to meet up that afternoon and visit the Kwame Nkrumah Memorial Park and Mausoleum in downtown Accra. I'd toured the landmark many times before but wanted to walk through the compound with Wemimo for the first time. I had a feeling its collection of precious memorabilia from Nkrumah's presidency, including the podium he stood on when he delivered his speech on Ghana's independence from Great Britain on March 6, 1957, would inform our conversation about Black Capitalism.

I met him in the lobby of the Marriott Hotel and we hailed one of the taxis waiting in the hotel driveway. Wemimo greeted me with his signature smile, but his slumped shoulders and quietness revealed how tired he was. "How are you feeling?" I asked while we sat in intermittent traffic. The end-of-year Esusu deliverables left him feeling burned out and exhausted. "All I want to do is sleep, which is so unlike me," he whispered with his eyes closed and head leaned back against the headrest. I felt sorry for him and promised to reserve my questions until we arrived at our destination, giving him time to rest.

As we pulled into the parking lot of the memorial, Wemimo's energetic demeanor returned as I woke him up from his thirty-minute nap. We meandered through the museum that stood behind the mausoleum. Wemimo, a history buff, shared historical tidbits about the men and women featured in the gallery. He spoke about Nkrumah, who was an inspiration to him because of his vision for Africa. "My desire to build a credit bureau system in Africa akin to what exists in the United States is in large part inspired by the vision Nkrumah set for the continent, which has yet to be realized," he told me while staring at a 1950s black-and-white image of Nkrumah standing alongside Chinese diplomats.

I watched him linger on the photo until he shared what the picture made him think about. "You know, Rachel, one thing that annoys me is that people gripe about how international players like China are coming in and taking advantage of the country, extracting resources, exploiting people, and running the country to the ground. But what people don't talk about is the fact that China has been part and parcel to Ghana's foreign relations development for a long time," he complained while still staring at the image.

I countered, arguing that imbalances in national power play a role in how countries can even engage with one another. Sangu's ideas about the negotiating power of one African country versus the unification of fifty-four countries were top of mind.

"With all of the attention on the country and continent now and multiple international stakeholders, there are options. [Ghana] is not the victim so many suggest while complaining about how international players are just manipulating the country as they see fit. And with options comes power and opportunity," he argued, adding that Ghana is now positioned to weigh those options and it is up to the leaders of the country to leverage and seize those opportunities wisely.

We talked about Ghana's growing social, political, and economic power as we looked at photos of Malcolm X, Maya Angelou, W. E. B. Du Bois, Marcus Garvey, Martin Luther King Jr., and Muhammad Ali. The occasional guided tour would pass by and steal my attention as I eavesdropped on group chatter.

As I listened to the people around us, I realized that two distinct conversations were happening simultaneously, each with its own historical starting point. One centered on the Atlantic slave trade and our collective need as Black people to return to the continent after enduring the vestiges of slavery. The other predated the slave trade in its focus on African royalty, commerce, and the continent's indelible influence on the Western world. Nkrumah's twentieth-century Pan-African renaissance, which captivated the attention of diasporans of his time, was just as relevant in the twenty-first century as I and the rest of the world watched the diaspora turn its gaze back to Africa.

We left the museum to walk past Nkrumah's sky-blue Cadillac Cruiser encased in glass and spotted a roaming peacock showcasing its luscious green, blue, and teal feathers near the still water pools filled with algae. Hiding from the sun, we sat on a cement bench under a neem tree, people watching and talking about Wemimo's practice of Black Capitalism.

"Capitalism is a construct that has always dealt with two classes of people—the bourgeois and the proletariat. We need a new capitalist structure where there are no winners or losers, which counters old economic theology," he explained. At Esusu, they're rethinking everything that we know and unlearning things from product development to customer acquisition and membership. The premise is to treat everyone as fairly and justly as possible to level the playing field. Wemimo was adamant about stopping what he calls "the game of pendulums." When in motion, a pendulum swings forward only to swing backward again—a constant interplay between progression and regression. History has proved that society will progress in one direction only to regress yet again—a vicious cycle leaving many behind who are most vulnerable to society's shifting moral compass. Hence the need for justice.

"We need to ask ourselves if what we are doing in business is both leveling the playing field for those who have been left behind and ensuring that everything we do is fair and balanced for everyone going forward," he noted. A strategy focused on equity and equality. "Everything we do in society today is at the crux of inequality. Black Capitalism is about the collective of people to reimagine what has been created." He argued that capitalism has been the most successful economic system but is crumbling bit by bit. It's everyday people who will create the groundswell needed to create change from the bottom up.

As he put it: "Change doesn't happen by making sure people that are comfortably positioned in society are bought in. It takes a movement of everyday people to make that change and regardless of the power held by the few, they ultimately fall in line because at the point of transformation, they have something to lose."

This chat with Wemimo would mirror a conversation I would have with Sangu a few weeks later over tacos at a Brooklyn dive bar. Like Wemimo, Sangu was unapologetic about his position as a Black Capitalist and held no reservations about his intent to acquire economic power to engender political power. He talked about understanding the many critiques of capitalism and his ideas about possible alternatives. But in the meantime, his resolve is to acquire as much economic power as possible since capitalism is the economic system we have today. "I don't have much patience for anti-capitalists who aren't interested in appreciating the importance of economic power in the current political economy. I've never met someone in poverty who wants to be poor. Who the fuck *wants* to be poor?" he griped.

Through his company, Sangu's participation in capitalism is an ethical approach to driving sustainability by investing in assets and companies focused on bettering people's lives through technology, healthcare, and access. He takes pride in the fact that stories of the businesses in which he invests are having tremendous impact on society in meaningful ways. "When MPharma announced we've worked with two hundred thousand–plus patients, that was incredible for me. When Nandela raised a hundred million dollars, the largest raise ever for Pan-African tech, that was huge. Making an impact in helping African students become Rhodes Scholars and knowing that their lives are forever changed is amazing," he said. He also established a fund at Peddie for supplemental financial aid to cover the hidden costs of elite preparatory schools like college visits and social events. "If I die today, the funds and scholarships I've set up will live on and the impact my business has made will do the same," he said. Using capital to change the life chances of people is the promise of Black Capitalism.

Wemimo's and Sangu's entrepreneurial journeys prove that there are productive ways to engage in a capitalist economy with the hopes of transforming it in ways that yield meaningful impact for the world's most marginalized people. Their ability to build businesses that nurture Black thriving forces us to reconsider the possible impacts of capital production. Though they are both critical of the shortcomings of capitalism, they forge ahead, determined to produce ethical value out of an imperfect system and improve the life chances of the economic majority rather than the elite minority.

In January 2022, Wemimo's startup, Esusu, hit unicorn status. After a second round of fundraising totaling $130 million, the seven-year-old fintech company now has a valuation of more than $1 billion.[1] This is a feat that only a handful of Black-owned startups globally have been able to accomplish. By December 2023, Esusu reported the creation of more than 107,000 new credit scores and more than $21.9 billion in capital unlocked for renters via new tradelines.[2] More than eight thousand evictions were prevented.[3] Mortgages totaling more than $14 billion became accessible, in addition to thousands of student loans and car loans for people who were once financially invisible.[4] Wemimo describes his work as "bridging the racial wealth gap by leveraging technology to create a permanent bridge to financial access and inclusion." Esusu is building a bridge to economic access, namely for immigrants and minorities in America, and a transatlantic bridge to Africa, given Esusu's cultural roots and long-term global vision to build credit visibility for the world's most financially invisible.

Wemimo's Black identity, and the fact of his having been thrust into poverty, influences how he uses capitalism's toolkit today. A sense of responsibility to marginalized people and their flourishing, alongside the dream of collective economic security, can be the telic cause for building a for-profit company with the tools of capitalism. This is one of many examples of how we can use the collective differences Audre Lorde talks about as our strength, which has the potential to catalyze change in the most unlikely of places.

My time in Ghana engaging with locals, diasporans, and entrepreneurs working at the helm of financial technology and innovation during the height of Ghana's cultural renaissance affirmed the groundswell of attention to and investment in Africa. But a driving question for Black Capitalists on African soil and in the transatlantic circuit is: How do we ensure that the value created on the continent benefits the communities who produce it? Doing so is essential to advancing social, political, and economic African power in the global marketplace, which in turn produces more opportunities for Black thriving to occur.

Investments are made with the intent to solve the most pressing social problems at scale, while also making a profit. For startup founders like Sangu who use their skills acquired on Wall Street, the prevailing challenge is to nurture scalable company cultures in Africa that thrive within a capitalist system but are distinct from the problematics of Western capitalism. Companies like CarePoint are doing the hard work of increasing the quality of life of their employees and creating business objectives that add value to people's lives in ways that advance Pan-African power building. They are using the tools of capitalism to produce global stories of Black thriving while making money doing it.

CHAPTER 11

An African Product, Made in America

These days I carry both my mom's American Dream and my Pan-African Dream with me. When I think back to the image of the man of color leaning against the graffiti wall that read, "EVERY MORNING I WAKE UP ON THE WRONG SIDE OF CAPITALISM," I'm reminded that every day I strive to be on the right side of capitalism—in both my practice of and relationship to it, in a world where many people find themselves on the wrong side. Capitalism as we know it treats laborers and natural resources, like clean air and uncontaminated water, as collateral damage as capitalists aspire to minimize labor costs and maximize profits. This fact is precisely why *this* story about Black Capitalists is both urgent and necessary. It gives us a new framework to consider how everyday Black people equip themselves to confront the trappings of capitalism with strategic ingenuity. Their methods and behaviors aim not to repeat the destructive practices of capitalism, but rather to use its tools to advance social good. There is no right side of capitalism until we make one, and *that* is the goal of Black Capitalism. This book holds space for the valid concerns that have a stronghold on our collective thinking while pushing us past them to reimagine the utility of capitalism, its actors, and range of impacts.

The tension attached to doing so leads to questions, especially when I consider my former work at JPMorganChase since the Supreme Court's rollback of affirmative action and its ripple effect in the industry. Do financial institutions hold no responsibility in correcting racial inequity, despite its part in advancing the racial wealth gap through the disproportionate collection of deposits and lag in lending (or extensive predatory lending) within Black and Brown communities? Should I not have benefited from the firm's homebuyer's assistance grant because I bought a home in a historically Black community that had long been divested due to recent gentrification? Or perhaps some of the Black business owners I know shouldn't have been approved for a loan for the first time in their lives because the firm loosened its restrictions on qualifying applicants? At surface level, the question everybody was asking was: Are these initiatives legal? But the deeper question at play was: Are Black and Brown people deserving of access to better lives after being denied it for so long? It was a loaded question that felt impossible to deny, and yet here we were considering it out of legal necessity. My employment at JPMorganChase gave me the knowledge to unlock a type of Black thriving even though it was unclear if the work that I was doing to help provide it for others could be achieved.

I found comfort in the firm's undercommons. A year before I joined the firm two Nigerian employees founded an organization called the African Alliance. Grappling with the unique challenges of being both Black and African at the firm, the co-founders built an informal, virtual space where people could seek connection, as well as personal and professional support. As soon as one of my Ghanaian colleagues told me about the collective after spotting me eating homemade red red in the staff kitchen, I got involved as an organizing committee member.

The monthly Zoom sessions we host corral more than one hundred African employees from across the firm globally for sessions that feel like group therapy. Some of the questions were: "How should I navigate people not understanding me because of my accent?" "What are some strategies on how to use your differences as a strength?" "I need to make a career move. What's your advice on pursuing internal mobility?" Some of the answers were: "You are held to a higher standard of performance than your peers. Make sure to strive for excellence in everything that you do." "Seek out mentors and sponsors, and know the difference between the two as you climb the corporate ladder." "Do not hide what makes you different. Lean into your differences because authenticity is attractive and pays off in the long run." From one month to the next, we bring our questions and concerns and leave with inspiration and the reminder that we are not alone, though that is the reality for many of us in our respective roles.

As I benefited from my involvement in the undercommons, I was prompted to ask myself: How do I also open doors for my external community to leverage JPMorganChase resources? The alliance's signature program, Africa Week, a series of nationwide events made for us and by us, was one opportunity I took advantage of. Instead of hiring the firm's catering services for our New York City event, I brought in African Restaurant Week and BedVyne Brew so that Black African–owned businesses could get JPMorganChase visibility for potential corporate catering opportunities in the future.

I had a dream to create the firm's first-ever African Film Festival, and within a year the NYC chapter of the African Alliance pulled it off. A Liberian friend in the entertainment world introduced me to Areej Noor, a Somali American who founded Statement, a data-driven entertainment startup that bridges the gap between African and diaspora women filmmakers and the international market. With her partnership and JPMorganChase funding, firm employees watched authentic African stories directed by young Black African women in the main auditorium of the firm's headquarters at 383 Madison Avenue. It was a sight to see because Black people's lived experience is hardly ever center stage in predominantly white institutions. Creating an event attended by more than a hundred people (and using JPMorganChase funds to do it) that engaged with humane portrayals of Black life interrupted the norm and solidified the belief that these stories should take up space within the walls of JPMorganChase.

Networking with other members of the African Alliance also led me to my current job as a researcher in the firm's Wealth Management Division. I had grown weary of doing DEI work that (in)directly called my humanity into question, and I needed a new challenge that aligned with my skill set as a researcher curious to find empirical solutions to social problems. In my current role I conduct ethnographic studies that help the firm develop products that meet the needs and behaviors of clients with money to invest. Historically, these clients have skewed predominantly white and wealthy. So the questions I ask myself while in this role are: What's the relationship between Black thriving and wealth management? What is JPMorganChase's role to play in that and how can I help facilitate that? How do I influence my stakeholders to apply a racial equity lens to the research we conduct and the products we develop? I learned from my previous role that nothing happens overnight. It's the strategic, slow-but-steady approach that's often needed to not only introduce these concepts but also build business goals around them. In the meantime, I make it my business to share with my community the knowledge I gain about investment fundamentals and financial health through the exposure of working at the largest bank in the country. I position myself according to the way my grandmother once taught me: You must give in order to receive in life. That is the bedrock of collective thriving.

Some of the questions we can all ask ourselves, no matter our position, are: What do I give? What do I receive? If you're a business owner or leader of an organization, you should wonder: What labor practices do I offer my team? Do those practices advance their well-being? If I were subject to the same practices, would I be able to thrive in life? As a professional in a corporate environment, what organizational structures do I challenge that limit or impede access to human thriving? Whatever we may be—a creative, a gig worker, a student, an investor, an innovator, an activist—we are all human. And so we should all be asking ourselves: How can I wake up on the right side of capitalism *and* make a way for others to do the same? The flow of resources cannot be one-directional in our favor. We are our own best bet to create the reality we hope for.

◆ ◆ ◆

An abundance mindset is both theory and practice. It requires us to believe that there are enough resources for everyone's fundamental needs to be met, which is the baseline for thriving. We must also trust that others who share this mindset will also give and receive resources in support of collective uplift, not just their own. To thrive alone implicates us in capitalism's individualism and moral bankruptcy. There is power, not weakness, in living life with the principle that we can't do it alone—we are interdependent.

When we embody an abundance mindset, we can lean into the vulnerable practice of excavating our economic trauma and the fear of not having enough or the threat attached to having too much. We're able to be honest about the fact that capitalism makes it hard for us to trust one another because we've been taught to value monetary gain over secure relationships with one another. How does a scarcity and abundance mindset show up in our everyday lives? One answer is in this final story.

It was summertime in New York and I was on the local C train headed toward Far Rockaway. The humidity made everyone look wet, sticky, and one more train delay away from irate. As a family of four with a stroller got off at the Utica Avenue stop, a spot opened by the train doors that offered the rare luxury of personal space. I made a beeline for it.

As during most of my commutes on the train, I had my earbuds in to give off the perception that I was occupied. But truthfully, I wasn't listening to anything on my phone; instead, I was listening to everyone around me. In front of me was a Black man with his three sons who looked to be anywhere between eight and thirteen years old. He looked young and athletic in his black Nike shorts and sneakers, gray Under Armour T-shirt, and drawstring backpack. Leaning against the end door, he held a large pizza box, a gallon of Coca-Cola, and four plastic cups as he talked to his children. "Back in the day you could get a big ass slice of pizza for a dollar and a soda for a few cents! Now you gotta pay five dollars just to get a slice. But I got each of us two slices and a drink for when we get to the park."

"You got money, Dad!" said his eldest son with a look of admiration.

He snapped in response, "Don't go telling people that shit! That's how you get robbed. You hear me? You don't need to know if I got money. I'm broke. You're broke. You hear me?"

Watching this father with his young, Black sons brought my mom to mind and the wisdom she imparted to me as a child. Both he and my mom were trying to protect their children with their knowledge about what money can do. What I heard in his words was the lesson that people are robbing one another in more ways than one, which reminded me of my mom's impulse to preserve my dignity when others denied me of it by having me clean the church building as a child. She taught me, just as this father was teaching his children, that money matters. The only people who say it doesn't are the people who have it. And even in the absence of you having money, it doesn't give people the right to make you their slave.

My attention cut to a Latina woman carrying a sleeping baby on her back as she boarded the train with a boy who appeared to be her preteen son. Subway riders made room for her and her family as she slowly and silently walked the length of the car hawking $2 World's Finest Chocolate bars stored in a makeshift cardboard box that she held with both hands. Some gave money in exchange for chocolate. Others just gave money.

As the train stopped and the woman moved on to the next subway car, three energetic Black teenage boys crowded in with a stereo in tow. "Ladies and gentlemen, it's showtime!" the hype man of the group announced. The buskers had their work cut out for them, as most passengers either looked vexed by the blaring music or ignored it completely. They did flips, spins, and impressive hat tricks around the silver car poles to little applause. But the lack of audience enthusiasm didn't curb their own. The performers gave it their best effort and finished with a synchronized bow that won over some people. Slumped in his seat, a middle-aged Black construction worker who looked like he'd had a long day of work extended his leg to reach into the pocket of his cement-stained pants for a dollar bill. A young Black boy with his school uniform and backpack on pulled some coins out of his pocket and dropped them in the olive-green trucker hat that doubled as the money bag. Funnily enough, the red embroidery on the hat read: "We Need More Black Billionaires."

These subway encounters reveal some of the brief and routine ways capitalism shows up in our everyday lives, how we respond to it, and in effect, how we relate to one another. They are also a reminder that capitalism exists beyond the boardroom. It's corporations, profit margins, and shareholders that make capitalism feel so extractive. Our economic system and the money that fuels it are supposed to support people so that they don't have to be in situations that challenge their ability to survive, much less thrive. Despite my time working in wealth management, it's the places of Black Capitalism, outside of conventional boardrooms, that I've seen provide us with a way to get free together. A crucial step in creating the right side of capitalism is to understand that we all have intrinsic value in who we are and how we live in community, not in what we can do or produce in the world.

ACKNOWLEDGMENTS

From the moment I embarked on writing this book, this section was the part I was most excited to write. To the people who shared their lives with me—this book is as much yours as it is mine. Thank you for your honesty and vulnerability.

This book wouldn't exist without my publishing team. Libby, Cierra, Annsley, and the other talented people at Crown, I am forever grateful for your thoughtfulness and attention to all the many elements that went into producing this book. Whitney, your instant curiosity and investment in sharing this book with the world has been a blessing to me. Hafizah Geter, you are a better agent than I could even think to ask for. Your brilliance, careful consideration of the topics in this book, advocacy, and humor made the difference. The fact that an anticapitalist and a capitalist-critic could find mutual value in telling this story gives me hope. Thank you for always going the extra mile and being better than good to me.

The scholars on my dissertation committee at Yale University were among the first to read initial drafts of this work. Douglas Rogers, Michael Ralph, Kathryn Lofton, Aimee Cox—your insightful edits, encouragement, and belief in my work helped me get it across the finish line. A special thanks to Michael for rocking with me since my NYU days. It's been a privilege to learn from and with you all these years.

Confidants of mine have spent hours speaking positivity over this work, reading drafts, and reminding me of its purpose in moments when I felt uncertain. Thank you for always being a guiding light. To my friends and chosen family, you've taught me the value and beauty of community. You've given me more than I could ever repay.

Nicolette Jaze, my favorite "work mom," thank you for pouring into the twenty-two-year-old version of me that was unsure of herself. Can you believe all that has happened since? Your steady love and support over the years have meant more than I could ever write here. You've positioned me to succeed countless times, and your engagement with this book has been no different.

My family is the best part of me. Dash, you are the first (and sometimes, only) person I share my dreams with. You've guarded them fiercely and sharpened them as if they were your own. Oh, how far we've come since Adams Drive. Mom, the older I get, the more I grow to admire you. Your strength and determination are unmatched. What you have done in this lifetime on behalf of your children and theirs will not go unnoticed. I count it a success if this book makes you both proud (and if I'm lucky, you'll grade it higher than a C, Mom). I love you. To my extended family back home, you inspire the boldness and bravery in me each and every day.

To God be the glory for it all.

NOTES

Introduction: Secure the Bag *and* the People

1. Students for Fair Admissions, Inc. v President and Fellows of Harvard College, U.S. Supreme Court, June 29, 2023, accessed June 20, 2024, https://www.supremecourt.gov/opinions/22pdf /20-1199_hgdj.pdf.
2. "Chairman and CEO Letter to Shareholders," JPMorganChase, last modified April 8, 2024, https://reports.jpmorganchase .com/investor-relations/2023/ar-ceo-letters.htm.
3. Ibid.
4. "Kwanzaa's Principles and Traditions," *New York Times*, last modified December 21, 2020, https://www.nytimes.com/2020 /12/21/dining/kwanzaa-seven-principles.html.
5. Lisa Lowe, *The Intimacies of Four Continents* (Durham, N.C.: Duke University Press, 2015).
6. Audre Lorde, "The Master's Tools Will Never Dismantle the Master's House," in *Sister Outsider: Essays and Speeches* (1984; repr. Berkeley, Calif.: Crossing Press, 2007), 110–14.
7. Introduced by Cedric Robinson, the Black radical tradition is a philosophical and political ideology that aggregates a collection of scholarship focused on the social, political, and

economic efforts of people across the world over time whose actions have served to disrupt social norms birthed in the colonial and slavery era.

8. Lorde, "The Master's Tools."
9. Ibid.
10. Ibid.
11. Within the literature on racial capitalism, the scholarship on race and racism also informs this story on Black Capitalists. Given the fluidity of race, scholars have struggled to agree on fixed terms that encompass racism's many features. It's why scholars have theorized multiple definitions of racism. Popular theories include color-blind racism, post-racism, and laissez-faire racism, to name a few. Key areas of focus within the scholarship on race and racism have included working-class populations and elites in various industries, as well as the relationship between racism and employer attitudes, work environments, corporate policies, and their impact on the stunted upward mobility of Black professionals.

Chapter 1: A Long Way from Adams Drive

1. Marcia Chatelain, *Franchise: The Golden Arches in Black America* (New York: Norton/Liveright, 2020).
2. Ibid.
3. Ibid.
4. Stefano Harney and Fred Moten, *The Undercommons: Fugitive Planning and Black Study* (Wivenhoe, U.K.: Minor Compositions, 2013).
5. Ibid.
6. Ibid.
7. *O.J.: Made in America*, directed by Ezra Edelman (ESPN Films, 2016), https://www.espn.com/watch/player?id=2840 463&_slug_=.
8. Stuart Hall, *Representation: Cultural Representations and Signifying Practices* (1997; repr. Thousand Oaks, Calif.: Sage, 2013), 272.

Chapter 2: The Spook Who Sat by the Door

1. W. E. B. Du Bois, *The Souls of Black Folk,* ed. C. Lemert (1903; repr. Boulder, Colo.: Paradigm, 2004), 55.
2. Ibid.
3. Ibid.
4. Ibid., 55–56.
5. Ibid., 56.
6. Ibid.
7. Ibid., 66.
8. Ibid.
9. Franz Fanon, *Black Skin, White Masks* (1952; repr. London: Pluto Press, 2008), 25.
10. Ibid., 4.
11. Ibid., 106.
12. Ibid., 178–79.
13. Ibid.
14. Ibid., 190–80.
15. Ibid., 179.
16. Kathryn Lofton, *Consuming Religion* (Chicago: University of Chicago Press, 2017), 233.
17. Laura Morgan Roberts and Ella F. Washington, "U.S. Businesses Must Take Meaningful Action Against Racism," *Harvard Business Review*, accessed April 27, 2022, https://hbr.org/2020/06/u-s-businesses-must-take-meaningful-action-against-racism.

Chapter 3: The Language of Black Capitalism

1. "Nipsey Hussle—Grinding All My Life," Genius, accessed June 19, 2024, https://genius.com/Nipsey-hussle-grinding-all-my-life-lyrics.
2. Juliet E. K.Walker, "Racism, Slavery, and Free Enterprise: Black Entrepreneurship in the United States Before the Civil War," *Business History Review* 60, no. 3 (1986): 371, https://www.jstor.org/stable/3115882.
3. Ibid., 341.

4. Ibid., 371.

5. Ibid., 367.

6. Ibid.

7. Ibid., 365.

8. Ibid.

9. Ibid.

10. Ibid., 369.

11. Ibid.

12. Ibid., 367.

13. Ibid.

14. Ibid.

15. Ibid.

16. Ibid., 369.

17. Ibid.

18. Ibid., 370.

19. Ibid., 364.

20. Ibid.

21. Ibid.

22. Juliet E. K. Walker, "Black Entrepreneurship: An Historical Inquiry," *Business and Economic History* 12 (1983): 38, http://www.jstor.org/stable/23702738.

23. Ibid., 38.

24. Mehrsa Baradaran, *The Color of Money: Black Banks and the Racial Wealth Gap* (Cambridge, Mass.: Belknap Press, 2017), 1.

25. Ibid., 7–11.

26. Ibid.

27. Ibid., 11.

28. Ibid., 26–27.

29. Ibid., 27.

30. Ibid., 30.

31. Ibid., 32.

32. Arnett G. Lindsay, "The Negro in Banking," *Journal of Negro History* 14, no. 2 (April 1929): 156, https://www.jstor.org/stable/2714067.

33. Ibid., 157.

34. Ibid., 201.

35. Baradaran, *The Color of Money*, 48.

36. Ibid.

37. Booker T. Washington, *The Future of the American Negro* (Boston: Small, Maynard & Company, 1899), 84–86.

38. Gil Kaufman, "Jay-Z Says There's No Shame in Success, Compares Being Called 'Capitalist' to the N-Word," *Billboard,* accessed September 2, 2022, https://www.billboard.com /music/rb-hip-hop-jay-z-twitter-spaces-interview-capitalist -n-word-1235134357/.

39. Kaufman, "Jay-Z."

40. "Hustle," *Oxford Advanced Learner's Dictionary*, accessed September 2, 2022, https://www.oxfordlearnersdictionaries .com/us/definition/english/hustle_1.

41. Isabella Rosario, "When the 'Hustle' Isn't Enough," NPR, last modified April 3, 2020, https://www.npr.org/sections/code switch/2020/04/03/826015780/when-the-hustle-isnt-enough.

42. Ibid.

43. Ibid.

44. "Rick Ross—Hustlin' (Official Music Video)," YouTube, last modified November 20, 2009, https://www.youtube.com /watch?v=JU9TourRn084.

45. "How to Properly Navigate the Gig Economy and the Large Pool of IT Experts," *Forbes*, accessed April 18, 2024, https:// www.forbes.com/sites/forbestechcouncil/2023/03/20/how-to -properly-navigate-the-gig-economy-and-the-large-pool-of -it-experts/?sh=2861d3d46794.

46. Ibid.

47. Ibid.

48. Ibid.

49. Oliver Large and PeiChin Tay, "Making It Work: Understanding the Gig Economy's Shortcomings and Opportunities," Tony Blair Institute for Global Change, accessed April 12, 2022, https://www.institute.global/insights /tech-and-digitalisation/making-it-work-understanding-gig -economys-shortcomings-and-opportunities.

50. "Quarter 3 2022 Labour Statistics Report," Ghana Statistical Service, last modified May 2023, https://statsghana.gov.gh /headlines.php?slidelocks=NTA0MDc2MTI5MS45MTE1 /headlines/883p6410nn.

51. Ibid.

52. Erin Griffith, "Why Are Young People Pretending to Love Work?," *New York Times*, accessed January 5, 2023, https://www.nytimes.com/2019/01/26/business/against-hustle-culture-rise-and-grind-tgim.html.

53. Ibid.

54. Ibid.

55. Ibid.

56. Tricia Hersey, "Rest Is Anything That Connects Your Mind and Body," Nap Ministry, last modified February 21, 2022, https://thenapministry.wordpress.com/.

57. Ibid.

58. Ibid.

59. Ibid.

60. Ibid.

Chapter 4: Champagne, Dice, and Everything Nice

1. Handulu bondibai is a Maldivian rice pudding.

2. Brianna Holt, "How Young Black Women Are Manifesting a Soft Life," *Insider,* accessed January 1, 2023, https://www.insider.com/how-young-black-women-are-manifesting-a-soft-life-2022-12.

3. Ibid.

4. Ibid.

5. Ibid.

6. Jadriena Solomon, "How to Start Living a Soft Life," *21Ninety,* accessed June 19, 2024, https://21ninety.com/how-to-start-living-a-soft-life.

7. L'Oreal Thompson Payton, "It's Time to Leave the Strong Black Woman Trope in the Past: Meet the Soft Black Girl," *Fortune,* accessed February 21, 2023, https://fortune.com/well/2023/01/15/black-women-soft-life/.

8. Ibid.

9. Elizabeth Ayoola, "Embracing Luxury as a Black Woman Has Been Hard—Here Is How I'm Shifting My Mindset," *Essence,* last modified February 17, 2022, https://www.essence.com/lifestyle/black-women-luxury/.

10. Tamara Morrison, "The Paradox of the Black Women in Luxury Movement," *Black Girls Around the World*, accessed January 2, 2024, https://blackgirlsaroundtheworld.com /2021/06/03/the -paradox-of-the-black-women-in-luxury -movement/.

Chapter 6: A Time After Black?

1. *O.J.: Made in America*, directed by Ezra Edelman (ESPN Films, 2016), https://www.espn.com/watch/ player?id=2840463&_slug_=.

2. Jay-Z, "The Story of O.J.," *4:44* (Roc Nation, 2017), 2017, accessed September 1, 2022, https://open.spotify.com/track /6JpN5w95em8SODPiM7W2PH.

3. "CNN O. J. Simpson Defense: 'If It Doesn't Fit, You Must Acquit,' " YouTube, accessed April 28, 2022, https://www .youtube.com/watch?v=NH-VuP_5cA4.

4. Stuart Hall, *Representation: Cultural Representations and Signifying Practices* (Thousand Oaks, Calif.: Sage, 2013), 236.

5. *O.J.: Made in America.*

6. Ibid.

7. Ibid.

8. Ibid.

9. Ibid.

10. Jay-Z, "The Story of O.J."

11. "Jay-Z & NFL Press Conference (Full Video)," YouTube, accessed April 28, 2022, https://www.youtube.com /watch?v=CpOzbPn-xDQ.

12. Jemele Hill, "Jay-Z Helped the NFL Banish Colin Kaepernick," *The Atlantic*, last modified December 17, 2021, https://www.theatlantic.com/ideas/archive/2019/08/jay-z -helps-nfl-banish-colin-kaepernick/596146/.

13. Brittani McNeil, "We Shouldn't Be Surprised by Jay-Z's NFL Move: He's Always Been a Capitalist and This Is What Capitalism Looks Like," *Black Youth Project*, last modified August 21, 2019, http://blackyouthproject.com/we-shouldnt -be-surprised-by-jay-zs-nfl-move-hes-always-been-a -capitalist-this-is-what-capitalism-looks-like/.

14. Hemal Jhaveri, "Jay-Z's Partnership with the NFL Is Just Another Reminder That Capitalism Always Wins," *USA Today*, last modified August 16, 2019, https://ftw.usatoday .com/2019/08/jay-z-nfl-kaepernick-is-just-another-reminder -that-capitalism-always-wins.

15. Kori Hale, "Sorry Kaep: Jay-Z's Commerce and Culture NFL Partnership Failure," *Forbes*, accessed August 22, 2019, https:// www.forbes.com/sites/korihale/2019/08/19/sorry-kaep-jay -zs-commerce-culture-nfl-partnership-failure/.

16. Derecka Purnell, "Jay-Z Has Crossed the Picket Line with His NFL Deal," *The Guardian*, accessed August 19, 2019, https:// www.theguardian.com/commentisfree/2019/aug/19/sorry -jay-z-racial-justice-corporations-billionaires.

17. Dave Zirin, "Jay-Z Isn't a Sellout, He's a Capitalist," *The Nation*, accessed August 20, 2019, https://www.thenation.com /article/archive/jay-z-kaepnerick-nfl/.

18. Ibid.

19. *Industry,* Season 1, HBO, https://www.hbo.com/industry.

20. *Industry,* episode 1, season 1, "Induction," HBO, https://www .hbo.com/industry.

21. Ibid.

22. Ibid.

23. Elizabeth Day, "Moritz Erhardt: The Tragic Death of a City Intern," *The Guardian*, last modified October 5, 2013, https:// www.theguardian.com/business/2013/oct/05/moritz-erhardt -internship-banking.

24. Julia La Roche, "A 22-Year-Old Goldman Sachs Analyst's Death Has Been Ruled a Suicide," *Business Insider*, accessed June 20, 2024, https://www.businessinsider.com/sarvshreshth -gupta-death-ruled-suicide-2015-6.

25. Ibid.

26. *Industry,* "Induction."

27. Ibid.

28. Ibid.

29. Ibid.

30. Ibid.

31. *Industry*, season 1, episode 8, "Reduction in Force," HBO, https://www.hbo.com/industry.

Chapter 7: Rebuilding the House

1. Aristotle, *Economics* (Rome: Aeterna Press, 2015).
2. Vanessa Romo, "Black Couple Settles Lawsuit Claiming Their Home Appraisal Was Lowballed Due to Bias," NPR, accessed August 17, 2024, https://www.npr.org/2023/03/09/11621032 86/home-appraisal-racial-bias-black-homeowners-lawsuit#:~: text=The%20lender%20agreed%20to%20send,higher%20than %20Miller's%20estimated%20value.
3. Audre Lorde, "The Master's Tools Will Never Dismantle the Master's House," in *Sister Outsider: Essays and Speeches* (Berkeley, Calif.: Crossing Press, 2007), 110–14.
4. Meek Mill (@MeekMill), "We in the easiest time to become a millionaire," Twitter, December 22, 2019, https://twitter.com /meekmill/status/1208943792033816576?lang=en.
5. *Gye Nyame* is an Akan expression that translates to "Except God."
6. "The Late Mr. Albert Mensah Snr.," *1st Annual Gha Awards,* 2015, 30.
7. Ibid.
8. Ibid.

Chapter 8: The Best Is Yet to Come

1. Spearheaded by Silicon Harlem (https://siliconharlem.com), the movement is committed to transforming Harlem and other urban markets into technology and innovation hubs that fully engage in the digital economy.

Chapter 9: Obroni

1. Africa Health Holdings is now CarePoint. The venture firm Golden Palm Investments still exists but now focuses exclusively on building Africa's technological infrastructure.
2. "Platform for Remittances, Investments, and Migrants' Entrepreneurship in Africa," IFAD, accessed June 20, 2024, https://www.ifad.org/en/prime-africa#:~:text=Remittances

%20sent%20by%20migrant%20workers%20to%20and,are%20 brought%20into%20the%20formal%20financial%20 system%2C.

3. TED Talk, "There's No Shame in Taking Care of Your Mental Health | Sangu Delle," YouTube, accessed June 20, 2024, https://www.youtube.com/watch?v=BvpmZktlBFs.

4. On occasion and without warning, the power goes out across neighborhoods in Accra. Although it's a frustrating phenomenon for most, Ghanaians will often make light of the loss of power with cheeky comments directed at the Ghanaian government for its failure to provide a consistent power supply to its citizens.

Chapter 10: An African Renaissance

1. Tage Kene-Okafor, "Esusu Becomes Unicorn with SoftBank Vision Fund 2-Led $130M Funding," TechCrunch, accessed March 7, 2022, https://techcrunch.com/2022/01/27/esusu -becomes-unicorn-with-softbank-vision-fund-2-led-130m -funding/.

2. "Esusu Renters," Esusu Rent, accessed June 20, 2024, https:// esusurent.com/press/esusu-renters-create-over-21-9-billion -in-new-credit-tradelines-and-establish-100k-credit-scores/.

3. Ibid.

4. Ibid.

INDEX

NOTE ON THE TYPE

The display typeface is set in Redaction, a typeface commissioned for painter Titus Kaphar and poet Reginald Dwayne Betts's *The Redaction* exhibition at MoMA PS1. Forest Young and Jeremy Mickel are the creators of the typeface. Redaction is considered a multiplicity of typographic, legal, and human histories. With a focus on social justice, *The Redaction* project aims to expose abuses in the criminal justice system experienced by poor, marginalized people who are imprisoned for failure to pay court fines and fees. Kaphar and Betts treated typography as a key element in the creation of this work. Betts, who is also a lawyer, produced original poems by redacting information from legal documents filed by the Civil Rights Corp, which was juxtaposed to Kaphar's portraits of individuals represented in the claims. This approach—the merger of text and legibility—inspired the development of a bespoke typeface that could animate the work and serve as a tool to raise awareness of the project at scale.

ABOUT THE AUTHOR

Rachel Laryea is a thought leader who specializes in race and money, ethical entrepreneurship, and social good. After cutting her teeth on Wall Street at Goldman Sachs, Rachel received her dual PhD in African American Studies and Anthropology at Yale University. Her ethnographic research aims to understand nuanced forms of Black participation in capitalist economies. Rachel is the recipient of the National Science Foundation Research Fellowship award and received an honorable mention from the Ford Foundation for her research. She has held adjunct professor appointments at the NYU Stern Business School and worked as a racial equity investment strategist at JPMorganChase. Currently, she is a wealth management researcher at JPMorganChase.

Rachel is the founder of Kelewele, a lifestyle brand based in Brooklyn, New York, that produces vegan, plantain-based treats and bespoke travel experiences. Kelewele has partnered with the James Beard Foundation and BET, and has been featured in several global publications and media platforms, including *Market-Watch*, *Forbes*, ABC, and CBS. She is the recipient of the Ghana UK-Based Achievement (GUBA) Award.

———————